CARD GAMES FOR ONE

No better amusement has ever been devised than a game of patience. In this book the author has collected 87 patiences—a number of old favourites, some lesser-known but nonetheless interesting games, and some new compositions that are appearing in print for the first time. The rules of each game are clearly described and the layout is illustrated wherever desirable.

As well as providing a novel glossary, Mr. Hervey introduces the reader to 41 single-pack patiences, 38 double-pack patiences and 8 new patiences, requiring more skill than luck, composed by Charles Jewell. All the best-known games are included from Demon, Sir Tommy and Miss Milligan to Clock and Senior Wrangler. . . . No bridge club is properly equipped without this book.

Sunday Telegraph

TEACH YOURSELF BOOKS

CARD GAMES FOR ONE

Patiences—Solitaires

George F. Hervey

ST. PAUL'S HOUSE · WARWICK LANE · LONDON EC4P 4AH

First printed 1965
Fifth impression 1973

ISBN 0 340 05538 3

*Printed by photolithography
for The English Universities Press Ltd at The Pitman Press, Bath*

CONTENTS

INTRODUCTION

A game of patience has many virtues. It sharpens the wits, it develops judgement, it helps the power of concentration and, in this way, assists in the development of that elusive quality which for want of a better name we call card sense. Above all, a game of patience has a great moral value because, when it is properly approached, it calls for the self-discipline of being honest with oneself. To cheat oneself at patience is said to be the hall-mark of the lowest form of human life. Withal it is understandable. There is much gratification in bringing a game of patience to a successful conclusion. If sometimes we strain the rules and exchange an obstinate card for a more manageable one, no one is the worse for it, and we can always salve our conscience with the thought that when everything has been said, it could have been this way in the shuffle.

Games of patience (solitaire)[1] are played either with one or two packs of cards. In a few patience games more than two packs are used, but they have been excluded from this book; for they are very cumbersome, even when played with the extra small packs especially made for patience players.

Most (though not all) games of patience follow a recognised pattern.

[1] The name solitaire is preferred by American card players. It is probably a better name than patience because it is more descriptive. I retain the name patience, however, because in this country the name of solitaire has been appropriated by a game played with marbles on a board.

The pack is shuffled, and in a double-pack patience the two packs are shuffled together.

The game usually begins by some or all of the cards in the pack being dealt to the board and arranged in a specified way. The primary object of the game is to release certain cards (usually the Aces) as foundations and on them build up the whole pack usually in ascending order of suit-sequences.

If all the cards are not dealt to the board at the beginning of the game, those left in the hand of the player are dealt either singly or in packets, and, according to the rules of the game, are played either to the foundation piles or to the exposed cards on the board or to a waste heap.

Games of patience fall into two natural groups: those played with a single pack and those played with a double pack. In the text this well-defined dividing line has been retained (games played with less than a full pack of fifty-two cards are treated as single-pack patiences) and within the two groups the games have been arranged in alphabetical order. The alphabetical arrangement, however, is largely one of convenience, and must be accepted for what it may be worth. It is not an ideal arrangement; for there is some inconsistency in the names that have been given to the games. For example, the Demon, so popular among British players, is equally popular among American players but under the name of the Canfield;[1] and what in America is called the Klondike is usually called the Canfield by British players. Many games have more than one name, indiscriminately used by players.

----

[1] So called because it was reputedly invented by Richard A. Canfield, a well-known New York gambler.

It is one of the disadvantages of a game of patience that skill accounts for only a small part of the play: in the majority of games success or failure depends very largely, sometimes entirely, on the fortuitous distribution of the cards. Such games can have no great appeal to those who take their card playing seriously. I have, therefore, added some selected games that have been composed by my friend Charles Jewell: all are double-pack games that call for thought, care and skill if the player is to succeed. Inevitably, however, and as in all card games, even contract bridge, the fortuitous distribution of the cards plays a big part, but it may fairly be claimed that in all his compositions the chance of success is not high, so that winning a game is at least an occasion for self-congratulation.

No author of a book about patience games ever escapes the criticism that his descriptions of the various games are hard to understand. That this is so is not altogether the fault of the author. The reader has to understand that a game of patience is not subject to hard and fast rules, like a game of bridge or some other scientific game, because a player is not competing against others for a stake. A game of patience may sometimes serve to pass away the time in sickness, an evening of weariness when no better entertainment is available, or it may be that the player aims to sharpen his wits by pitting his judgement and power of observation against the pack. It is proper, therefore, that the author does no more than give a general outline of the way to play some particular game and leave it to the individual to determine the details for himself. With no authoritative body, such as there is for bridge and many other games, the reader is not asked to follow unbreakable rules, but merely to obey the general principle described in the text, making such variations as he chooses in the number of times that he deals the stock, the transfer of a sequence from one card in the lay-out to another, and the like, so as to conform best with the circumstances that prompted the game.

By definition games of patience are designed for one player only. A large number of patiences, however, can be played competitively. Many are. Crossword, Golf and Poker are patiences that are particularly suitable for competitive play, and the older generation may well remember that some half century or more ago Poker patience played competitively was all the rage; matches were played, tournaments were held, and even leagues were formed. Then, too, we must not forget the famous Racing Demon, that the Americans call Pounce, which was, if it no longer is, played as a hilarious round-game by any number of players up to a dozen. Each has his own pack of cards and plays a game of Demon (Canfield) building his cards to any foundation pile on the board. Speed is essential (and long finger nails do much damage to hands) since the winner is the one who first disposes of his stock regardless.

On the whole, however, the present writer does not applaud the introduction of the competitive element into games of patience. He believes that it is more proper to approach them in the same spirit that "Sarah Battle" approached the game of whist. He leaves it at that.

GEORGE F. HERVEY   *Bagshot*, 1965

DEFINITIONS

Blocked. A game is blocked when no card can be played to or from the lay-out, or no move made within the lay-out, in accordance with the rules of the game.

Board. The table or other surface on which the game is played.

Build. To place a card in sequence on a foundation in accordance with the rules of the game.

Centre. A generic name for the foundations.

Column. Two or more cards played to the board, each immediately below another.

Exposed Card. A card at the foot of a column, at the end of a row, or elsewhere, which may be moved, built on or packed on, in accordance with the rules of the game.

Fan. Two or more cards placed on the board side by side, each slightly overlapping its neighbour.

Foundation. A card played to the centre of the board on which other cards are built, usually in ascending order of suit-sequence.

Heel. A number of cards placed in a pile on the board to be played as directed by the rules of the game.

Lay-out. The cards dealt to the board at the beginning of a game and arranged in a pattern according to the rules of the game.

Pack. To place a card in sequence on an exposed card in the lay-out in accordance with the rules of the game.

Round the Corner. A sequence in which the Ace connects the top and bottom of the suits, i.e. . . . J Q K A 2 3 . . .

Row. Two or more cards played to the board side by side.

Sequence. Two or more cards, not necessarily of the same suit, that follow each other in ascending or descending order of pip value.

Stock. The cards left in the hand of the player after the original lay-out has been dealt to the board.

Waive. To lift a card in order to be able to play one under it.

Waste Heap. Cards played from the stock and set apart in a pile as they cannot be played by the rules of the game either to the foundations or the lay-out.

Worry Back. To return cards, already played to the foundations, to the lay-out.

SINGLE-PACK
PATIENCES

AGNES

DEAL to the board twenty-eight cards face upwards in a row of seven cards, then a row of six cards, then a row of five cards, and so on (dealing one card less each time) to a row of one card. For convenience the cards in each row may slightly overlap the cards in the previous one. The twenty-ninth card is dealt to the centre to indicate the foundations.

The object of the game is to build ascending, round the corner suit-sequences on the four foundation cards.

The bottom card of each column in the lay-out is exposed. It is available to be played either to a foundation or to be packed in descending sequence of the same colour but not necessarily of the same suit. A sequence may be transferred from one column to another as a whole provided all the cards in the sequence are of the same suit. If a space occurs, by reason of all the cards in a column being moved, it may, but not necessarily must, be filled by any exposed card or by a sequence of cards of the same suit.

Suppose the original lay-out is as shown on page 3.

As the Sixes are foundation cards, indicated by the 6♠, the 6♢ is played to the centre alongside it. Now the Q♡ is packed on the K♢, and the J♡ on the Q♡; the 2♠ is packed on the 3♣; and so on.

When all possible moves have been made, a card is dealt from the stock face upwards to the bottom of each column, and the game continued in this way until the stock is exhausted. At the third deal from

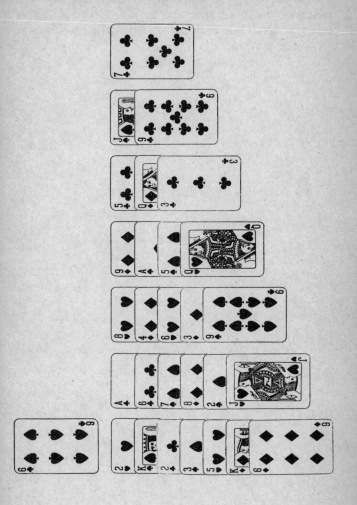

the stock to the lay-out there will be two cards in excess of the seven necessary to play to the columns; both are available for play either to the foundations or to the lay-out.

REMOVE from the pack the two black Aces and the two red Kings, and place them to the centre of the board as foundation cards.

The object of the game is to build ascending sequences of alternate colours on the two black Aces to the two black Kings, and descending sequences of alternate colours on the two red Kings to the two red Aces.

The stock is dealt one card at a time, and if a card cannot be built on a foundation it is played to a waste heap. The player is allowed four waste heaps, to which he plays the cards at his discretion. The top cards of the waste heaps are always available for play.

When the stock is exhausted the player collects the four waste heaps in any order he chooses, and without shuffling deals the stock a second time. Only two deals of the stock are allowed.

BELEAGUERED CASTLE

REMOVE the four Aces from the pack and place them in a column to serve as foundations. Deal face upwards six cards on each side of the four Aces. For convenience the cards in the rows may slightly overlap.

The object of the game is to build ascending suit sequences on the four foundations, from Aces to Kings.

Only the extreme left-hand and right-hand cards of each row are exposed. They may be packed in descending sequence irrespective of suit or colour, or may be moved either to a foundation card or to another exposed card in the lay-out. Only one card may be moved at a time. When a space occurs by reason of all the cards on one side of an Ace having been moved, it may be filled by any exposed card from the lay-out.

Suppose the original lay-out is as shown on page 7.

The 2♡ (row D) is built on the A♡, exposing the 8♠ which may now be packed on the 9♣ (row B) exposing the Q♢. The J♢ (row D) may be packed either on the Q♣ (row C) or the Q♢ (row D). The 5♣ (row A) may be packed on the 6♠ (row A), the 4♠ (row B) on the 5♣, and the 3♣ (row C) on the 4♠. And so on.

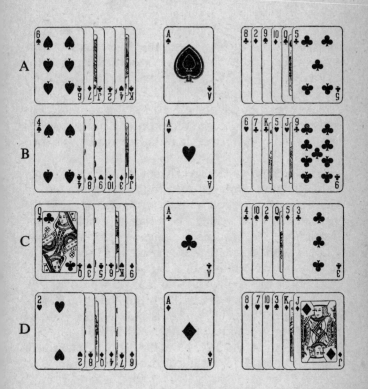

BISLEY

DEAL the entire pack face upwards in four rows of thirteen cards each, placing the four Aces on the extreme left of the top row. As the four Kings become available in play, they are moved to a row above their respective Aces.

The object of the game is to build ascending suit-sequences on the Aces and descending suit-sequences on the Kings. It does not matter where the two sequences meet.

The bottom card of each column is an exposed card. It may be moved to a foundation, packed on the exposed card of another column, or itself be packed on. Packing may be either in descending or ascending suit-sequence, which the player may change at his convenience. A space left vacant in the lay-out by the removal of a card is not filled.

Suppose the original lay-out is as shown on page 9.

The 2♣ and 3♣ are built on the A♣; the K♣ is played to the centre; the 2♦ is built on the A♦, as also are the 2♥ and 3♥ on the A♥. The 6♥ and 7♥ are packed on the 5♥. Now the 10♦ is packed on the J♦, and the K♠ played to the centre. Etc. etc.

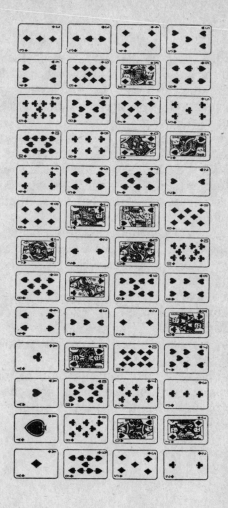

BLIND

ONE card, known as the blind, is dealt face downwards to the board. Seven cards are then dealt to the board face upwards in a row as the lay-out. Aces, as they occur in play, are played to the centre of the board as foundations.

The object of the game is to build ascending suit-sequences on the foundations from Aces to Kings.

The stock is dealt one card at a time, and any card that cannot be played to a foundation must be played to one of the cards in the lay-out, at the discretion of the player.

Only the top cards, for the time being, of the seven piles in the lay-out are exposed and available for play to the foundations. The player may always inspect the piles before making a play.

When a space occurs in the lay-out, by reason of all the cards of one pile being played to the foundations, the space must be filled either with the exposed card from one of the other piles, or with the next card from the stock.

The blind card is turned and brought into play only when the run of the game is stopped and the stock is exhausted. Only one deal is permitted.

Twenty-four cards are dealt face upwards to the board in eight fans of three cards each. Kings are placed at the bottom of the fans in which they occur. Aces as they become available are played to the centre as foundations.

The object of the game is to build ascending sequences, irrespective of suit and colour, on the foundations from Aces to Kings.

The top card of each fan may be played to the foundations or packed in descending sequence irrespective of suit and colour. Only one card may be moved at a time. When all the cards in a fan have been moved, the space in the lay-out is not filled.

The stock is dealt three cards at a time, one card to each of three waste heaps. Only one deal is allowed.

CALCULATION

REMOVE any Ace, any Two, any Three and any Four from the pack and place them on the board face upwards in a row to form the four foundations. The object of the game is to build the remaining forty-eight cards in the pack on them. For this purpose the Ace counts as 1, the Jack as 11, the Queen as 12 and the King as 13.

On the Ace-foundation the cards are built in the order: A, 2, 3, 4, 5, 6, 7, 8, 9, 10, J, Q, K. On the Two-foundation they are built in the order: 2, 4, 6, 8, 10, Q, A, 3, 5, 7, 9, J, K. On the Three-foundation they are built in the order: 3, 6, 9, Q, 2, 5, 8, J, A, 4, 7, 10, K. On the Four-foundation they are built in the order: 4, 8, Q, 3, 7, J, 2, 6, 10, A, 5, 9, K. Suits are ignored.

After the four foundations have been laid on the board, the cards in the stock are dealt one at a time, and every card must be played either to a foundation or to a waste heap, of which there are four, one below each foundation. A card may be played to any one of the four waste heaps. The stock may be dealt only once, but play from the waste heaps may continue after the stock has been exhausted. A card in a waste heap may be played only to a foundation and must not be moved from one waste heap to another. Only the top card of a waste heap is available for play.

As an example:

Foundations	A ♦	2 ♡	3 ♡	4 ♠
Waste Heaps	A	B	C	D

The player turns up a Six from the stock. He plays it to the Three-foundation. Next he turns up a Seven. The card cannot be played to a foundation so he plays it to waste heap A. Next comes a Four. This is played on the Two-foundation. Next comes a King. As the King is the last card to be played to a foundation, Kings should be kept at the bottom of waste heaps. It would be bad tactics, therefore, to play it to waste heap A and so cover the Seven; it would be better to play it to waste heap B, and there are some players who would now reserve this waste heap for Kings. The play continues in this way until the stock is exhausted.

The patience is well-named; for it is necessary to calculate at every turn of a card. The experienced player aims at playing cards to the waste heaps (if they cannot be played to the foundations) in the reverse order to which they are built up on the foundations. If this is correctly thought out and calculated at each turn of a card from the stock, towards the end of the game, the player will find that when he moves a card from a waste heap to a foundation, he will be able to make several more moves.

CARPET

REMOVE the four Aces from the pack and play them to the centre as foundations.

Deal to the board twenty cards face upwards in four rows of five cards each.

The stock is turned one card at a time to one waste heap, and the game ends when the stock has been exhausted.

The object of the game is to build ascending suit-sequences on the four Aces up to the four Kings.

Only cards in the lay-out and the top card of the waste heap may be played to the foundations. When a card is played from the lay-out to a foundation the space in the lay-out must be filled with the top card of the waste heap. If, however, there is no card in the waste heap, it is filled with the top card of the stock.

CLOCK

DEAL forty-eight cards face downwards in twelve piles of four cards each, and arrange the piles in a circle on the board corresponding to the figures on the dial of a clock.

Take the top card of the stock, and, counting the Jack as 11 and the Queen as 12, place the card face upwards under the pile of its number and remove the top card of the pile. Place this card face upwards under the pile of its number, remove the top card and continue in this way until a King is turned up. When this occurs the King is played to a waste heap and the game is continued with the next card of the stock, until the stock is exhausted.

The object of the game is to end with twelve piles of four cards of the same rank, and the four Kings in the waste heap. It is obvious that success will come only if the last card to be turned up is a King. This so rarely occurs that if the fourth King is turned up before the game is won, it is permitted to exchange it for one of the face-downward cards in the lay-out and continue the game. Only one exchange may be made.

CROSS-WORD

THE top card of the pack is dealt face upwards to the board. The rest of the pack is dealt, one card at a time, and each card is placed on the board in any position so long as it touches (either at the top, bottom, either side or one of the four corners) a card previously played to the board.

The object of the game is to make a square (seven cards each way) in which the pips of the cards in each row and column add up to an even number. The court cards are not counted; they serve as stops and correspond to the black squares in a cross-word puzzle. The pips of the cards between the stops must, of course, also add up to an even number.

When forty-eight cards have been played to the board there will be one space to fill and four cards left in the stock. A first-class win is scored if the player can complete the game with the top card of the stock. If he cannot he must try for a second-class, third-class or fourth-class win by trying to complete the game with the second, third or fourth card remaining in the stock.

DEMON

THE Demon is probably the best-known of all the one-pack patience games. In America it is usually known as the Canfield, so called because it was reputedly invented by Richard A. Canfield, a well-known gambler of the late nineteenth century. It was his practice to sell the pack to the player for $52.00 and pay $5.00 for every card in the foundation row when the game came to an end. It has been estimated that he stood to win about $25.00 every game. It was, however, not as lucrative as it may appear on the surface because for every punter Canfield had to employ a croupier to keep an eye on him during play.

Thirteen cards are dealt face downwards in a pile as a heel, and the top card is turned face upwards. Four cards are dealt face upwards in a row to the right of the heel, and the eighteenth card is dealt face upwards to the centre to indicate the foundations. As they become available the other three cards of the same rank are played to the centre as foundations, and the object of the game is to build ascending, round-the-corner suit-sequences on the four foundation cards.

The four cards to the right of the heel are packed in descending sequences of alternate colour. The bottom card of the four columns is always available to be played to a foundation, but sequences can be transferred from one column to another only as a whole. When a space occurs, by reason of a whole

17

column having been moved, it must be filled at once
with the top card of the heel, and the next card of the
heel is turned face upwards. When the heel is exhausted, spaces are filled from the waste heap, but
there is no longer an obligation to fill the space at
once.

The stock is turned in batches of three cards. If at
the end of the stock there is less than three cards they
are turned singly. The stock is dealt and redealt until
either the game is won or lost because no further
move can be made.

The chance of winning a game is estimated to be
one in thirty, but chances of success are improved by:

1. Dealing the thirteen cards of the heel face upwards in a column.

2. Not filling a space at once.

3. Transferring a part-sequence from one column
to another.

DIVORCE

DEAL the pack one card at a time face upwards to any one of four waste heaps. Aces and Twos, as they are dealt, are played to the centre as foundations.

The object of the game is to build ascending sequences of alternate colour and rank on each of the eight foundation cards. Thus the red Aces are built up to red Kings by way of a black Three, a red Five, a black Seven, a red Nine and a black Jack; and the black Aces are built up to black Kings by way of a red Three, a black Five, a red Seven, a black Nine and a red Jack. By the same token, the black Twos are built up to red Queens by way of a red Four, a black Six, a red Eight and a black Ten, and the red Twos are built up to black Queens by way of a black Four, a red Six, a black Eight and a red Ten.

The pack may be dealt only once.

DOUBLETS

DEAL to the board twelve packets of three cards each face downwards and cover each packet with a card face upwards. Lay aside the remaining four cards face downwards.

Any two exposed cards of the same rank are discarded, and the next cards under them in the packets are turned face upwards. When a space occurs, by reason of all four cards of a packet having been discarded, it is filled by a card drawn from the stock.

The object of the game is to discard the whole pack in pairs.

DEAL forty-eight cards face upwards to the board in eight columns of six cards each. The cards in the columns may for convenience overlap. The remaining four cards are retained in hand to form the start of a reserve.

The object of the game is to release the Aces, play them to the centre as foundations and build on them ascending suit-sequences up to the Kings.

The cards in the reserve and the cards at the foot of each column are exposed, and may either be played to the foundations or packed in descending suit-sequences either with a card from the reserve or a card from the bottom of a column. Only one card may be moved at a time. The exposed cards in the lay-out may at any time be taken into the reserve, but the reserve must never exceed eight cards in all.

If a space occurs in the lay-out, by reason of all the cards in a column being moved, the space may be filled only by a King.

FLORENTINE

DEAL five cards face upwards to the board in the form of a cross. The sixth card is dealt to the centre to denote the foundations, and the other cards of the same rank will be played to the centre as they occur.

The object of the game is to build ascending, round-the-corner suit-sequences on the four foundation cards.

Suppose the original lay-out is as on the facing page.

The 7♡ is the foundation card, and the 7♠, 7♢ and 7♣ will be played to the centre of the board as they occur, and built up to their respective Sixes.

The four outer cards of the cross are packed in round-the-corner, descending sequences irrespective of suit or colour. When one of these cards is played to a foundation or packed on another card of the cross, the vacant space may be filled either with the top card from the waste heap or with the card from the centre of the lay-out and the centre space filled with the top card from the waste heap. The card in the centre of the lay-out must not be packed on.

The stock is dealt one card at a time, and one redeal, without shuffling, is allowed.

FLOWER GARDEN

THIS is generally considered to be one of the most interesting of the many one-pack patience games, because success is not entirely the result of the fortuitous order of the cards.

Fan out on the board six packets of six cards each face upwards. They are known as the beds. The remaining sixteen cards in the pack are retained in the hand. They are known as the bouquet.

The object of the game is to release the four Aces, play them to the centre as foundations, and build on them in ascending suit-sequences up to the Kings.

All sixteen cards in the bouquet are exposed and may be played either to a foundation or to a bed. Only the outer card, for the time being, of a bed is exposed. It may be played to a foundation, or packed on in descending sequence irrespective of suit and colour. A sequence may be transferred from one bed to another provided the sequence is retained.

If a bed is cleared, the vacant space may be filled either by a card from the bouquet, or by an exposed card or sequence from another bed.

FIVE rows of seven cards each are dealt face upwards to the board, to form what is called the links. The cards in the rows may overlap. The top card of the stock is played face upwards to the board. On it may be played the bottom card of any one of the seven columns of the links, provided it is next in sequence either upwards or downwards. Play continues in this way until no further card can be played from the links, or the run is brought to an end by playing a King; for though a player may build upwards or downwards at his discretion the sequences are not round-the-corner so that a King stops a run. The next card is dealt from the stock and play continues until all seventeen cards of the stock have been dealt, or the game has been won by the player clearing all the cards from the links.

KING ALBERT

DEAL forty-five cards face upwards to the board in
nine columns beginning with a column of one card
and, increasing each column by one card, ending
with a column of nine cards. The cards in the
columns may overlap. The remaining seven cards
(called the Belgian Reserve) are retained in the
hand. The bottom card of each column and all the
cards in the reserve are exposed. As the four Aces
become available they are played to the centre
as foundations.

The object of the game is to build ascending suit-
sequences on the foundations from Aces to Kings.

The exposed cards at the foot of the columns are
packed in descending sequences of alternate colour.
Only one card may be moved at a time. Worrying
back is permitted. When all the cards of a column
have been moved, the available space may be filled by
any exposed card.

KLONDIKE

TOGETHER with the well-known Demon (*see* p. 17) Klondike is one of the best-known and most popular of one-pack patience games. In this country it is usually called the Canfield. It is a misnomer; for Canfield is no more than the name that the Americans have given to the Demon patience.

Deal to the board twenty-eight cards face downwards in a row of seven cards, then a row of six cards, then a row of five cards, and so on (dealing one card less each time) to a row of one card. The rows may overlap. The bottom card of each column is then turned face upwards, as in the diagram on page 28.

Aces, as they become available, are played to the centre as foundations, and the object of the game is to build ascending suit-sequences on them up to the Kings.

The face-upwards card at the bottom of each column is available to be played to a foundation, or it may be packed in a descending sequence of alternate colour. A sequence may be moved from one column to another only as a whole. When a face-upward card or sequence is moved so that a face-downward card is cleared that card is turned face upwards. When a whole column is cleared the space may be filled only by a King with or without a sequence attached to it. Thus in the illustrative diagram, the 5♡ in column B may be packed on the 6♠ in column A, and the face-downward card at the foot of column B

27

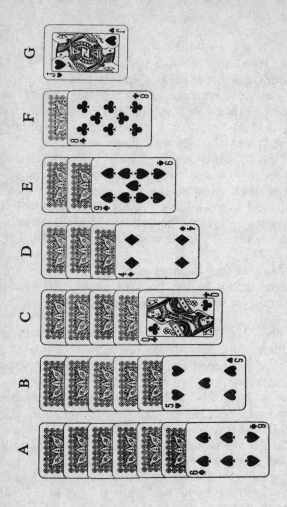

is turned face upwards; the J♡ in column G may be packed on the Q♣ in column C, and when a King is available it may be played to the space in column G.

The stock is turned one card at a time to a waste heap, the top card of which is available for play to a foundation or to the lay-out. Only one deal is allowed.

An Ace must be played to the centre as soon as it is available, but with all other cards the player has the right to leave them *in situ* in the prospect of finding a better move for them later in the game.

LABYRINTH

REMOVE the four Aces from the pack and play them
to the centre as foundations. Deal to the board eight
cards, face upwards in a row, as the lay-out. Any
appropriate cards in the lay-out are moved to the
foundations, and when all moves have been made, the
spaces left vacant are filled with cards from the stock.

The object of the game is to build ascending suit-
sequences on the Aces up to the Kings.

Three rows of eight cards each are dealt below the
first row. After dealing each row the player moves
appropriate cards to the foundations, and spaces
left vacant by moving cards to the foundations are
not filled (except in the case of the initial row) with
cards from the stock.

Exposed cards, that may be moved to the foundations, are those in the top and bottom rows, and, of
course, when a card is moved to a foundation from
either of these rows it exposes the card in the row
immediately below or above it.

Suppose that after the fourth row has been dealt
the lay-out is as shown at the head of the facing page.

Now the 2♣ and 2♡ may be moved to their
foundations from row D. As a result the 3♣ in row C
and the 3♠ in row B are exposed and may be moved
to their foundations. Now the 4◇ in row B and the
5◇ in row A may be moved to their foundation;
the 4♠ in row A and the 5♠ in row D; the 4♣ in
row C, the 5♣ and 6♣ in row A; and the 6◇ in
row B.

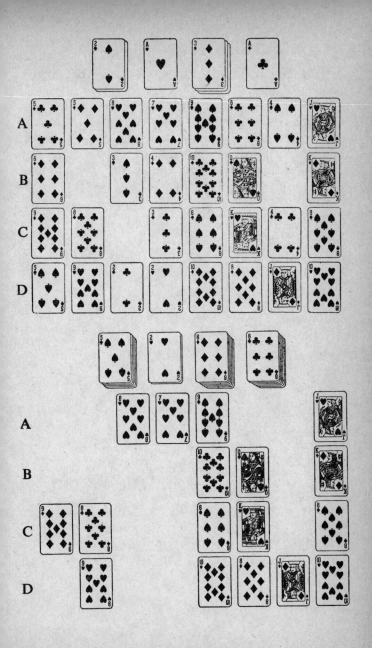

The lay-out is now as shown at the foot of the previous page.

A fifth row of eight cards is now dealt to the lay-out and when all moves have been made a sixth row.

If after the stock has been exhausted a block occurs, the player is entitled to waive by moving any one card he chooses from the lay-out to a foundation.

REMOVE the four Aces and play them to the centre as foundations.

Deal the remaining forty-eight cards to the board in twelve columns of four cards each, the first and third cards of each column face downwards, the second and fourth cards face upwards.

The object of the game is to build ascending suit-sequences on the four Aces to the four Kings.

The bottom cards of the twelve columns are exposed. They may be built on the foundations, or packed on the exposed cards of the lay-out in descending sequences of alternate colour. A sequence may be moved as a whole, or in part, from one card in the lay-out to another, but when a space in the lay-out occurs, because all the cards in one column have been moved, it may be filled by only one card. Cards that are dealt to the lay-out face downwards are turned face upwards when all the cards below it have been cleared.

MAZE

SOME consider that Maze is by far the best of the one-pack patiences; for though it does not always succeed it will, far more often than not, if the play is skilful.

The whole pack is dealt face upwards to the board in two rows of eight cards each and then four rows of nine cards each. The four Kings are discarded from the lay-out to leave four spaces, or six spaces in all because the two spaces at the end of the first two rows are taken into the lay-out for play.

The object of the game is to arrange the forty-eight cards—moving them one at a time into the available spaces—into four ascending suit-sequences from Ace to Queen, beginning with an Ace at the extreme left of the top row, and ending with a Queen at the extreme right of the bottom row. The sequences, of course, follow on from the end of one row to the beginning of the row below it, as in reading and writing.

A card may be moved into a space provided it is in suit-sequence one higher than the card on the left of the space or one lower than the card on the right of the space. For this purpose not only is it assumed that the rows are continuous, but that the bottom row is continuous with the top row. When a space occurs on the right of a Queen it may be filled with any Ace as an alternative to the card one lower in suit-sequence than the card on the right of the space.

In order to illustrate the mechanics of the game, we

may suppose that after the four Kings have been discarded the lay-out is:

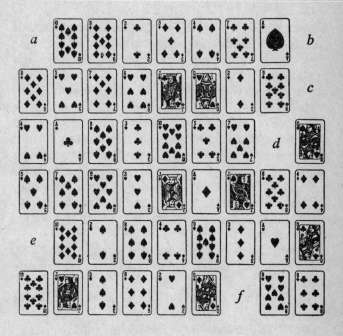

Space a may be filled with any Ace, or the 9♠ by reason of the 10♠ on the right of the space, or the 7♣ by reason of the 6♣ at the end of the bottom row.

Space b may be filled either with the 2♠ or 7♦.

Space c may be filled either with the 10♣ or 3♥.

Space d may be filled either with the 8♥ or J♠.

Space e may be filled either with the 5♦ or 9♦.

Space f may be filled by any Ace or the 8♥.

MONTE CARLO[1]

DEAL to the board twenty cards face upwards in four rows of five cards each. Any two cards of the same rank that are touching each other, either at top and bottom, at side and side, or at corner and corner, are discarded. When all possible discards have been made, the lay-out is consolidated by closing up the rows from right to left and from a lower row to the row above it, retaining the cards in the same order as they were dealt. When all the cards remaining in the lay-out have been closed up, the lay-out is completed with up to twenty cards dealt from the stock.

The game continues until the stock is exhausted, and won if the player succeeds in clearing the board. A win is very rare.

If three cards of the same rank touch each other, the player may choose which of the two he will discard.

Suppose the original lay-out is as on the facing page,

Move 1. Discard the 6♠ and 6♣ in column A.

Move 2. Discard the 4♡ in column A and the 4♢ in column B.

Move 3. Discard the 9♡ in column B and the 9♠ in column C.

Move 4. As no more discards are possible close the rows and complete the lay-out with six

---

[1] A double-pack variation of this game has been composed by Charles Jewell. Under the name of Pair Fives it is described on p. 137.

A   B   C   D   E

cards from the stock to replace the discards . . .

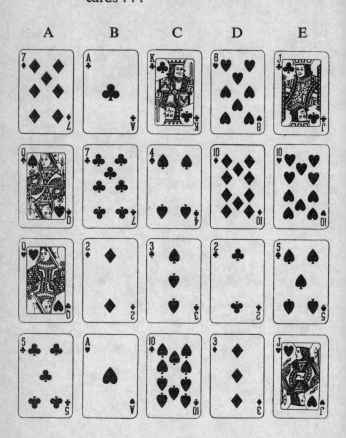

A　　　B　　　C　　　D　　　E

Move 5. Discard the 7♦ in column A and the 7♣
in column B. Etc., etc., etc.

NINETY-ONE

THE game is not a difficult one, but it may be fairly described as a vexatious one to those who cannot do simple addition without the help of their fingers.

The whole pack is laid out on the board in thirteen packets each of four cards face upwards.

The top card of each packet may be moved to another packet, thereby exposing the card under it and covering the top card of the packet to which it is moved. Counting Kings as 13, Queens as 12, Jacks as 11 and the remaining cards according to their pip value, the object of the game is for the player to so move the top cards of the packets until they total exactly ninety-one. A complete sequence from Ace to King fills the bill, and there are many other combinations that will.

Assume that the top cards of the thirteen packets are: 4♣, 7♦, 8♣, Q♠, 7♡, 5♡, 4♦, K♣, J♠, 4♡, 6♣, 10♡, 2♠.

The total is ninety-three, and it is, therefore, necessary for the player to lose two. He lifts the Ten of Hearts and finds underneath the Six of Spades. He has lost four, but by placing the Ten of Hearts on the Eight of Clubs he gains two. The lay-out is now: 4♣, 7♦, 10♡, Q♠, 7♡, 5♡, 4♦, K♣, J♠, 4♡, 6♣, 6♦, 2♠, and the total is ninety-one. Ichabod!

ONE FOUNDATION

THIRTY-FIVE cards are dealt face upwards to the board in five rows of seven cards each, each row slightly overlapping the one above it. The thirty-sixth card is dealt to the centre as the only foundation card.

The object of the game is to build the whole pack on the foundation card. An Ace must not be built on a King, nor a King on an Ace, otherwise the player may build in an ascending or descending order irrespective of suit or colour, and at any time he may change from building an ascending sequence to a descending one, and vice versa.

Only the bottom card for the time being of the seven columns in the lay-out are available for building on the foundation card.

When no further play can be made from the lay-out to the foundation, the next card of the stock is dealt to the foundation and built on. Play continues in this way until the stock is exhausted or the game has been won.

POKER

THE top card of the pack is dealt face upwards to the board. The rest of the pack is dealt, one card at a time face upwards, and each card is placed on the board in any position so long as it touches (either at the top, bottom, either side or one of the four corners) a card previously played to the board.

The object of the game is to make a square (five cards each way) to form poker combinations in each row and each column.

The poker combinations, together with the score for them, are:

Straight Flush, 30 points, five cards of the same suit in sequence the Ace either high or low, but not round-the-corner.

Fours, 16 points, four cards of the same rank and an odd card.

Straight, 12 points, five cards in sequence the suits immaterial, the Ace either high or low, but not round-the-corner.

Full House, 10 points, three cards of the same rank and two other cards of the same rank.

Threes, 6 points, three cards of the same rank and two odd cards.

Flush, 5 points, any five cards of the same suit.

Two Pairs, 3 points, two cards of the same rank, two other cards of the same rank, and an odd card.

Pair, 1 point, two cards of the same rank and three odd cards.

The maximum score is 230 points, but a win may be counted if 75 or more points are scored.

PUSS IN THE CORNER

REMOVE the four Aces from the pack and place them face upwards on the board in a square. They serve as foundations, to be built on in ascending colour-sequences (not necessarily suit-sequences) up to the Kings.

The stock is dealt one card at a time, and if a card cannot be played to a foundation it is played to a waste heap. Four waste heaps are allowed, and by tradition they are placed at the four corners of the foundation-square.

If the game fails to succeed before the stock is exhausted a second try (but only one) is allowed. The four waste heaps are gathered in any order and re-dealt without shuffling.

PYRAMID

DEAL face upwards to the board twenty-eight cards in seven rows, beginning with a row of one card and increasing each row by one card so that the seventh row will be of seven cards. Arrange the cards in the form of a pyramid, so that every card (except those in the bottom row) is overlapped by two cards in the row below it. In this way the removal of two adjacent cards in a row will expose a card in the row above it.

The object of the game is to discard Kings singly and other cards in pairs that together add to thirteen (a Queen counting as 12 and a Jack as 11). Only exposed cards may be discarded and the game is won if the whole pack is discarded.

The stock is turned one card at a time to a waste heap. The top card of the waste heap is exposed and may be paired with the next card turned from the stock or with any exposed card in the lay-out.

Suppose that the original lay-out is as shown on the facing page.

Now the Q♠ and A♣ (12+1=13) and the K♡ in row G may be discarded. It exposes the J◇ in row F which may be discarded with the 2◇ in row G thus exposing the 5♠ in row F, and so on.

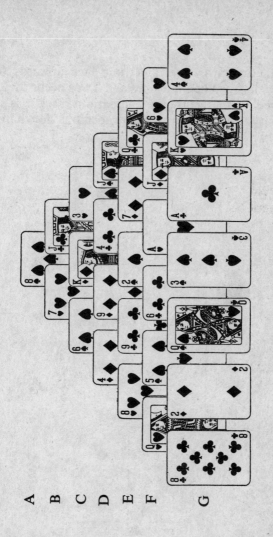

QUADRILLE

DEAL the cards one at a time face upwards to a waste heap. When the Aces and Twos occur they are played to the centre as foundations, and it is customary to arrange them in the positions shown in the following diagram.

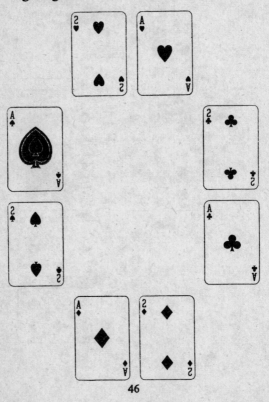

The object of the game is to build on the foundations ascending suit-sequences, odd cards (3, 5, 7, 9, J, K) on the Aces, and even cards (4, 6, 8, 10, Q) on the Twos.

If the game is successful, the lay-out will exhibit each King with his Queen on his right, in the same positions, that is, as the eight dancers at the beginning of a quadrille.

Two redeals (three deals in all) are allowed, but the waste heap must not be shuffled between deals.

RAGLAN

REMOVE the four Aces from the pack and play them to the centre as foundations.

Deal to the board as the lay-out forty-two cards in seven rows, the first row of nine cards, the second of eight cards, and so on down to a row of three cards. The rows may overlap. The remaining six cards is the stock.

The object of the game is to build ascending suit-sequences on the foundations from Aces to Kings.

The bottom cards for the time being of each column are exposed. They may be played to the foundations or packed in a descending sequence of alternate colour on the other exposed cards in the lay-out. The six cards in the stock are exposed also; they may be played either to the foundations or to the exposed cards in the lay-out but may not themselves be played on. Exposed cards must be moved singly; a sequence may not be moved as a whole. When a space occurs in the lay-out, because all the cards of a column have been moved, it may, but not necessarily must, be filled with an exposed card.

Suppose the lay-out is as shown on the facing page. The 2♠ from the stock is moved to the foundation, as also is the 3♠ from row B and the 4♠ from the stock. The 5◇ in row A is moved to the 6♠ in row G, the 6♡ in row A is moved to the 7♠ in row E. The K♣ in row C is moved to the space in row A or B. Now the 5♠ in row B, followed by the 8◇ in row A can be moved to make another space. And so on.

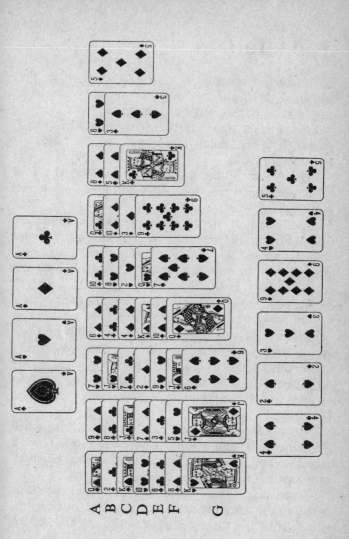

SCORPION

DEAL to the board a row of seven cards, four face downwards and then three face upwards. Deal two more rows in this way, and then four rows face upwards. For convenience the rows may overlap each other. The remaining three cards of the pack are retained in hand.

The object of the game is to pack on the four Kings within the lay-out descending suit-sequences to the Aces.

The cards at the bottom of each column are exposed and the next lower card in suit-sequence may be packed on them. For this purpose a card may be taken from anywhere in the lay-out, but all the cards below it in the column must be moved with it.

Suppose the lay-out is as shown on the facing page.

The 4♠ in column E may be packed on the 5♠ at the foot of column A, but the 6♠, 10♣ and 6♢ must be moved to column A with the 4♠. In the same way the 5♡ in column C may be packed on the 6♡ at the foot of column B, but the J♣ must be played to column B with it. And so on. Nothing can be packed on an Ace.

When a face-downward card is cleared it is turned face upwards, and when a whole column is cleared the available space is filled by a King together with any cards below it in the column.

When no further moves can be made, the three cards in the stock are dealt face upwards, one card to the foot of the three columns at the extreme left of the lay-out. The game is continued until it succeeds or is again blocked.

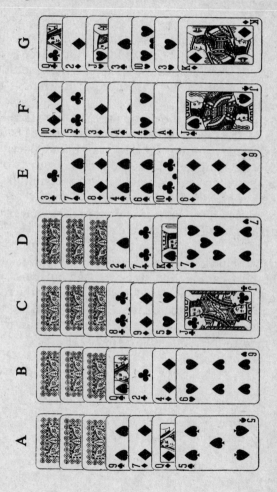

SEVEN UP

SEVEN UP is probably the simplest of all patience games. In fact it has been said that if a player is not half asleep and has a knowledge of simple addition and multiplication, he will succeed in winning the game nine times out of ten.

The player deals the cards one at a time face upwards to the board. When a Seven is dealt it is discarded, and, counting the Jack as 11, the Queen as 12, and the King as 13, when the pips of any two or more consecutive cards total seven or a multiple of seven they are discarded.

The object of the game is to discard the whole pack.

Suppose the first four cards dealt are: 8♠, 3♢, 6♡, Q♡. The 3♢, 6♡ and Q♡ are discarded as their pip value is $3+6+12=21=7\times3$.

The next card of the stock is dealt to the board alongside the 8♠. Suppose it is the 6♣. As the total pip value of the two cards is $8+6=14=7\times2$ the two cards are discarded and the player starts again from scratch with the remaining cards in the stock.

SIMPLE SIMON

DEAL face upwards to the board the whole pack in eight overlapping rows, the first row of ten cards, the second of nine cards, and so, decreasing by one card each row, to an eighth row of three cards.

The object of the game is to build within the lay-out descending suit-sequences on the Kings to the Aces.

The bottom card of each column is exposed and may be packed in descending sequence irrespective of suit and colour. Only one card may be moved at a time from one exposed card to another, but a sequence may be moved as a whole provided that all its cards are of the same suit. A space made by clearing all the cards from a column may be filled by any exposed card or sequence if all the cards of it are of the same suit.

Suppose the lay-out is as shown on page 54.

The 9♠ in column J is packed on the 10♠ in column B, the 3♢ in column I is packed on the 4♢ in column E, and the 10♡ in column H on the J♣ in column C. Now the 10♠ and 9♠ in column B are packed on the J♠ in column H and the Q♢ in column B is moved to the space in column J. Etc. etc.

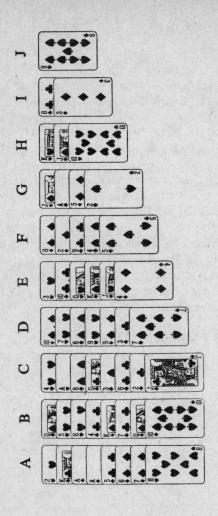

SIR TOMMY—LADY BETTY

SIR TOMMY is sometimes called Old Patience, because it is believed the first of all patience games from which all the others have been derived.

Inevitably, therefore, the game could hardly be simpler. The cards are dealt face upwards one at a time, playing Aces as they occur to the centre as foundations, to be built up in ascending sequences to the Kings regardless of suit and colour, and other cards either to the foundations or to four waste heaps (Sir Tommy) or six waste heaps (Lady Betty) at the discretion of the player.

Only one deal is allowed, and a card once played to a waste heap cannot be moved to another.

SPACES[1]

DEAL face upwards to the board the whole pack in four rows of thirteen cards each. The Aces are removed from the positions they occupy in the lay-out; they take no part in the game. The removal of the four Aces leaves four spaces in the lay-out which are used for beginning the play.

The object of the game is so to arrange the cards that each row consists of one suit, beginning with the Two and ending with the King. No particular row is singled out for any special suit; the player makes his own decision, and, having made it, must stand by it.

Play begins by moving into the spaces that have been left by the removal of the Aces, the next higher cards of the same suit as the cards on the left of the spaces. That is to say, if the order of a row is . . .

$$5\clubsuit \quad 6\diamondsuit \quad - \quad J\spadesuit \quad 8\heartsuit \quad 5\heartsuit \quad \text{etc.}$$

the space must be filled with the $7\diamondsuit$ and not with the $10\spadesuit$.

Only one card may be moved at a time.

It is obvious that the filling of one space leaves another. This is filled in the same way, and so on, until the run of the game is stopped by the positions of the four Kings.

Three tries are permitted. When the first and second tries come to an end, all the cards in the lay-out that are out of sequence are collected and shuffled. They are then dealt to reform the lay-out, for the second

[1] A double-pack variation of this game has been composed by Charles Jewell. Under the name of Paganini it is described on p. 132.

and third tries, by dealing the cards to the board with a space in each row to the immediate right of the cards that are already in sequence.

This patience has the merit of being one of the very few in which the fortuitous order of the cards is less important than the player's skill. The player has to look ahead; for with four spaces to fill (each releasing a card, and it when moved releasing another card, and so on) much depends upon the order in which the player fills the four available spaces.

STAR

REMOVE the twelve court cards from the pack.

Deal to the board twelve cards face upwards in a column of one, a column of three, a column of four, a column of three, and a column of one, as shown in the diagram on the facing page.

The object of the game is to exhaust the stock by covering any two cards in the lay-out that together total eleven with two cards drawn from the stock.

Nearly always a wide choice of moves is available. Thus, in the accompanying diagram the player may cover the 2♣ with the 9♠, 9◇ or 9♡, the 6♠ either with the 5♡ or 5♣, and so on. Which two cards to cover must be decided before drawing cards from the stock.

STRATEGY

REMOVE the four Aces from the pack and put them temporarily aside. Deal eight cards face upwards to the board in a single row, as eight waste heaps. Deal the rest of the pack one card at a time face upwards, and play each card to one or other of the eight waste heaps. When the whole pack has been dealt, play the four Aces to the centre as foundations. The top card of each waste heap is available for play, and the object of the game is to build ascending suit-sequences on the foundations from Aces to Kings.

THIRTY is played with the short or piquet pack (i.e. a pack from which the Twos, Threes, Fours, Fives and Sixes have been removed) sometimes called the thirty-two-card pack.

Deal to the board thirty cards face upwards in six rows of five cards each, each row overlapping the previous one. The two remaining cards are retained in hand. They are treated as exposed cards and are available to play to the foundations or the lay-out. The bottom card of each column is an exposed card. Aces, as they become exposed, are played to the centre as foundations.

The object of the game is to build suit-sequences on the Aces up to the Kings, beginning the sequence by playing the Seven on the Ace.

Exposed cards in the lay-out may be played to the foundations, or they may be packed in descending sequences irrespective of suit and colour. A sequence, or any part of one, may be transferred from one column to another, provided the highest card of the sequence so transferred is next lower than the exposed card to which it is played.

When all the cards of a column have been played, the vacant space may be filled by an exposed card or sequence of cards.

THIRTY-SIX

DEAL to the board thirty-six cards face upwards in six rows of six cards each, each row overlapping the previous one. Only the bottom card of each row is exposed.

Any exposed Aces, or Aces as they occur in the play, are moved to the centre as foundations.

The object of the game is to build ascending suit-sequences on the Aces up to the Kings.

Exposed cards in the lay-out may be played to the foundations, or may be packed in descending sequences irrespective of suit and colour. A sequence, or any part of one, may be transferred from one column to another, provided the highest card of the sequence so transferred is next lower than the exposed card to which it is played.

When all the cards of a column have been played, the vacant space may be filled by an exposed card or sequence of cards.

After the first thirty-six cards have been dealt to the board, and all available plays have been made, the stock is turned one card at a time. If the card turned cannot be played to a foundation or to the lay-out, it is played to a waste heap, the top card of which is always available for play.

Only one deal is allowed.

TOWER OF HANOY

THIS patience is one that has the merit of not being difficult and very convenient to play since only nine cards are used. With the small cards made for patience games it can be played in the confined space of a railway carriage, to the infuriation of one's fellow-travellers who go mad trying to work out the rules of the game.

Remove from the pack nine cards from Ace to Nine inclusive. They need not be all of the same suit, though tidyness demands that it is better if they are. Shuffle them and deal them to the board in three columns of three cards each.

The object of the game is to arrange the cards in one column with the Nine at the top in downward sequence to the Ace.

The following rules govern the movement of the cards.

1. Only one card must be moved at a time.

2. Only the bottom card of a column may be moved.

3. A card may be moved only to the foot of another column and only if the card at the foot of that column is higher in rank to the card that is being moved.

4. When any column is void of cards a new column may be started by moving the bottom card of either of the two remaining columns to form the top card of the new column.

Suppose that the original lay-out is:

Move 1—3♡ to column A.
Move 2—2♡ to column A.
Move 3—5♡ to column C.
Move 4—4♡ to column C.
Move 5—2♡ to column B.
Move 6—3♡ to column C.
Move 7—2♡ to column C.
Move 8—9♡ to column B.

The lay-out is now as shown on the facing page.

The 9♡ is in position, and the player has to work to get the 8♡ below it, then the 7♡, and so on down to the A♡.

A B C

WINGS

DEAL thirteen cards face downwards in a pile as a heel. On each side of it deal four cards face upwards in a row. Deal the next card face upwards to the centre to indicate the foundations. As cards of the same rank become available they are played to the centre as foundations; the object of the game is to build ascending, round-the-corner suit-sequences on the four foundation cards.

The stock is turned one card at a time to a waste heap. The top card of the waste heap and the eight cards in the wings are available to be played to the foundations. When a card has been played from the wings to a foundation its place is filled by the top card of the heel. When the heel is reduced to one card it is turned face upwards and may be played direct to a foundation without having first to be played to a wing. When the heel is exhausted spaces made in the wings, by playing cards to the foundations, may be filled either from the waste heap or the stock.

When the stock has been dealt it may be redealt twice (three deals in all) without shuffling.

DOUBLE-PACK
PATIENCES

ALHAMBRA

REMOVE from the pack one Ace and one King of each suit, and play them to the centre as foundations.

The object of the game is to build ascending suit-sequences on the Aces to the Kings, and descending suit-sequences on the Kings to the Aces.

Deal to the board face upwards thirty-two cards in eight packets of four cards each. The stock is turned one card at a time and any card that cannot be played to a foundation is played to a waste heap. The top cards of the eight packets are exposed; they are available to be played to the foundations or to the waste heap, the top cards of which may be packed in ascending or descending round-the-corner suit-sequences. A space made by moving all four cards of a packet is not filled.

The stock may be turned three times in all.

ALTERNATION

DEAL seven cards face upwards in a row, below them seven cards face downwards in a row, then seven cards face upwards, and so on until seven rows of seven cards each have been dealt to the board, the first, third, fifth and seventh face upwards, the second, fourth and sixth face downwards. For convenience each row may slightly overlap the one above it.

The object of the game is to play the eight Aces to the centre as foundations and build on them in ascending suit-sequences to the eight Kings.

The bottom cards of the seven columns are exposed, and are packed in downward sequences of alternate colours. Sequences, or any part of one, may be moved from one exposed card in the lay-out to another.

When a move results in a face-downwards card occurring at the foot of a column it is turned face upwards.

Suppose that the original lay-out is as shown on page 70.

Now the 2♡ in column A is played to the 3♠ in column D and both are played to the 4◇ in column F. The A♣ in column B is played to the centre as a foundation, and the 10◇ in column G is played to the J♣ in column E. The cards face downwards at the foot of columns A, B, D and G are now turned face upwards and become exposed cards.

When all moves in the lay-out have been made, a

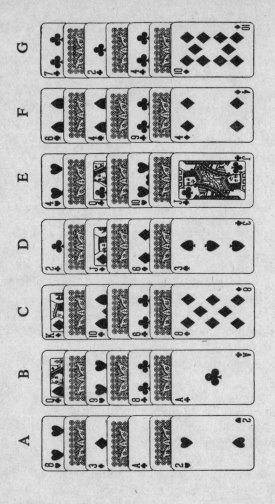

A   B   C   D   E   F   G

card is dealt from the stock and may be played either
to a sequence in the lay-out or to a foundation. If it
cannot be played to either, it is played to a waste
heap.

If all the cards in a column are moved, the space
left vacant may, but not necessarily must, be filled
with an exposed card or sequence from another part
of the lay-out, or with the top card of the waste heap.

The game ends when all the cards in the stock have
been dealt.

BABETTE

DEAL face upwards to the board a row of eight cards; below it deal another row, and so on until the stock is exhausted, but pausing after dealing each row in order to play available cards from the lay-out to the foundations.

The object of the game is to play one Ace and one King of each suit to the centre as foundations, and build ascending suit-sequences on the Aces to Kings, and descending suit-sequences on the Kings to Aces.

A card is exposed, and available to be played from the lay-out to a foundation, when its lower edge is free, that is to say if the card is at the bottom of a column or immediately above a gap in a column. In the diagram shown on page 73 the 3♡ and 6◇ in the top row are exposed as also are all the eight cards in the bottom row.

Before dealing a fourth row of eight cards, the 2♡ is played to the A♡ (exposing the 7♣) and the 3♡ is played to the 2♡.

When these moves have been made another row of eight cards is dealt to the lay-out; for a space made by playing a card from the lay-out to a foundation is not filled.

One redeal is allowed. When the stock is exhausted, the cards remaining in each column are slid into piles and picked up from right to left to remake the pack.

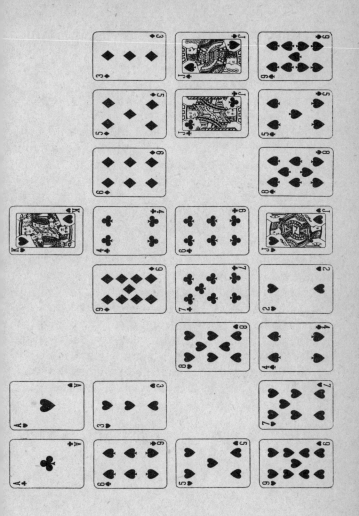

COLORADO

DEAL to the board twenty cards face upwards in two rows of ten cards each. As they become available play to the centre as foundations one Ace and one King of each suit.

The object of the game is to build ascending suit-sequences on the Aces to the Kings, and descending suit-sequences on the Kings to the Aces.

The stock is turned one card at a time, and if the card cannot be played to a foundation it is played to one of the twenty cards in the lay-out, irrespective of suit, colour or rank. In effect, the twenty cards in the lay-out are twenty waste heaps. The top card of each of these waste heaps is available to be played to a foundation, and when all the cards of a waste heap have been played to the foundations, the vacant space must be filled by the top card of the stock. A card cannot be moved from one waste heap to another, but only from a waste heap to a foundation.

The stock is dealt only once, and a card must not be dealt from the stock until the previous card has been played either to a foundation or a waste heap.

THE first forty-one cards of the pack are dealt face upwards to the board in the form of a diamond. That is to say, they are dealt in nine rows, the first and last row consisting of a single card, the second and eighth rows of three cards each, the third and seventh rows of five cards each, the fourth and sixth rows of seven cards each and the fifth row of nine cards.

The object of the game is to play the Aces to the centre as foundations and to build ascending suit-sequences on them to the Kings.

Unusually there is no packing on the cards in the lay-out; they may be used only for building on the foundations, with the restriction that only those cards with at least one free side (not top or bottom) are available to be played.

Suppose the original lay-out is as shown on page 76.

Clearly the only cards available for play are the K♠ in row A, the 6♢ and 2♡ in row B, the 9♣ and 5♡ in row C, the 2♣ and J♣ in row D, the 2♠ and 7♣ in row E, the Q♠ and 7♠ in row F, the A♠ and K♣ in row G, the 8♢ and 4♣ in row H and the J♠ in row I. As a result the A♠ in row G is played to the centre as a foundation (freeing the 9♢) and the 2♠ in row E is built on it (freeing the 3♢).

When all possible moves have been made from the lay-out, the stock is turned one card at a time, and any card that cannot be played to a foundation (for the moment the spaces in the lay-out are not filled)

A

B

C

D

E

F

G

H

I

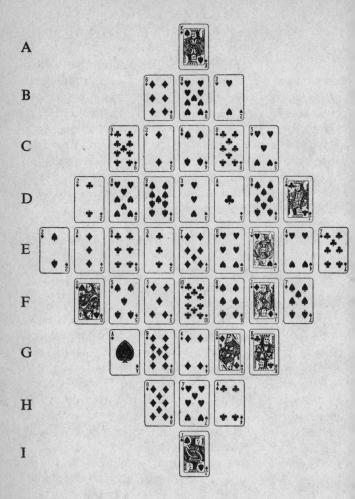

is played to one or other of three waste heaps. The player, however, has no choice to which waste heap to play a card: the waste heaps must be fed in turn from left to right. The top card of a waste heap is, of course, always available to be played to a foundation, and if there is a choice between playing a card to a foundation either from a waste heap or from the lay-out, the player may play whichever is the more convenient.

When the stock is exhausted, the player takes up the left-hand waste heap and uses the cards to fill any spaces in the lay-out. He may fill the spaces in any order he chooses, but he must not play any of the cards to a foundation. If there are insufficient cards in the waste heap to fill the spaces in the lay-out cards are taken from the middle waste heap.

When all spaces in the lay-out have been filled, the cards in the waste heaps are shuffled and dealt under the same rules as above.

A third deal under the same rules is allowed. At the end of it, however, if the game has not succeeded, the cards in the lay-out as well as those in the waste heap are shuffled together and a fourth deal played, the player first dealing to the board a diamond of twenty-five cards, namely a single card, a row of three cards, a row of five cards, a row of seven cards, then a row of five cards, a row of three cards and finally a single card.

DIEPPE

REMOVE the eight Aces from the pack and play them to the centre as foundations.

The object of the game is to build ascending suit-sequences on the Aces to the Kings.

Below each of the eight Aces deal a card face upwards to the board. If any card can be played to a foundation the space is filled with a card from the stock. When all moves, if any, have been made, a second and then a third row of cards are dealt in the same way. For convenience the rows may overlap.

After the three rows have been dealt, and by reason of moving cards to the foundations all spaces filled, the cards in the third row may be packed in descending sequences irrespective of suit and colour, and may themselves be packed on each other.

Consider the lay-out on the facing page. The 5♣ in column B may be packed on the 6♦ in column G. This exposes the Q♡ in column B which may be packed on the K♦ in column D, and either the J♦ in column C or J♠ in column F may be packed on the Q♡. And so on.

A sequence may either be moved as a whole or in part, and when a column has been cleared the space may be filled with any exposed card or sequence of cards.

The stock is turned one card at a time, and any card that cannot be built on a foundation or packed on the lay-out is played to a waste heap. Only one deal is allowed.

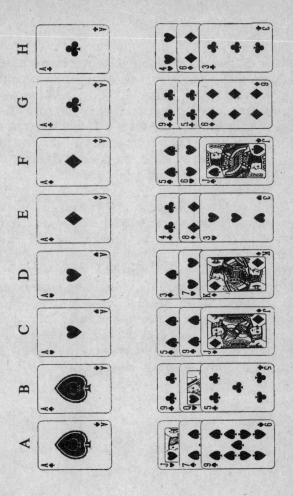

DISPLAY

DEAL face upwards to the top left-hand corner of the board the first card of the pack. Assume, for explanation, that it is a Five. The pack is now dealt one card at a time, and when the Four of any suit is dealt it is played to the right of the Five, a Three is played to the right of the Four, a Two to the right of the Three, and so on. When a Six is dealt it is played below the Five, a Seven below the Six, an Eight below the Seven, and so on.

The object of the game is to arrange all 104 cards in round-the-corner sequences, irrespective of suit and colour, each row of thirteen cards and each column of eight cards.

No card can be played to the lay-out unless the previous one is in position; unplayable cards are dealt to one or other of three waste heaps, the top cards of which are exposed and available to be played. When the pack is exhausted, the waste heaps are gathered and the pack redealt but with only one waste heap. Only two deals are allowed.

REMOVE from the pack one Ace and one King of each suit and play them to the centre as foundations. The object of the game is to build ascending suit-sequences on the Aces to the Kings, and descending suit-sequences on the Kings to the Aces.

The first twelve cards of the pack are dealt face upwards to the board and the thirteenth card is set aside face downwards to a heel. The deal is continued in this way until the whole of the pack has been dealt to form twelve face-upwards packets and one face-downwards heel. Whenever a card is dealt to a packet the player calls "Ace" for the first packet, "Two" for the second packet, and so on to "Jack" for the eleventh packet and "Queen" for the twelfth. If there is a co-incidence (that is to say, if an Ace is dealt to the Ace-packet, a Two to the Two-packet, and so on) the card is not played to the packet but face downwards to the heel, and the next card of the pack is dealt face upwards to the packet instead. As only one co-incidence is allowed to each packet, the packet itself should then be turned diagonally to indicate that no further co-incidence is allowed.

After the whole pack has been dealt, the top card of the heel is taken up and, according to its rank, the appropriate packet is taken in hand and sorted. Cards in appropriate sequence are played to the foundations; the rest may be arranged in any order that the player chooses. The packet is then replaced on the board horizontally to show that it has been sorted; for a packet may be lifted and sorted only once. If a second card of the same rank is drawn from the heel, the player may lift and sort the first unsorted packet beginning with the Ace-packet. If a King is drawn from the heel the player may lift and sort any packet he chooses, provided, of course, it has not already been sorted. If any cards are left in the heel after all the packets have been sorted, the cards left in the heel are turned face upwards and are available to be played to the foundations.

Throughout the game the top card of a packet is always available to be played to a foundation.

EIGHT AWAY

REMOVE any one King from the pack and play it face upwards to the board. Deal cards on it face upwards, overlapping, until a King occurs. Place this King to the right of the first one, and deal cards on it as above. Continue in the same way until the eight Kings are in a row and the whole of the pack dealt on them. That each King will have a different number of cards dealt on it does not matter.

The object of the game is to release the eight Aces, play them to the centre as foundations, and build on them ascending suit-sequences up to the Kings.

The bottom card of each column is exposed and may be packed in descending sequence of alternate colour. At any stage of the game the player may take into his hand from the lay-out any number of cards up to eight, but never more than eight, as a reserve. The cards may be taken only from the bottom of the columns; those already played to the foundations cannot be taken into the reserve. The cards may be held in reserve while other moves are made, and returned to the lay-out when convenient to the player.

A sequence may be moved as a whole from one exposed card to another, but a part-sequence may be moved only by taking cards into the reserve (never exceeding eight in hand at one time) and reconstructing the sequence. When a column is cleared the space is not filled.

EIGHTS

REMOVE from the pack a complete suit and arrange the thirteen cards face upwards in a row, from the Seven on the left to the Six on the right, to serve as foundations.

The object of the game is to build seven cards in sequence (irrespective of suit and colour) on the thirteen foundation cards, so that if successful there will be thirteen packets of eight cards each topped by a sequence from Ace to King.

The stock is dealt one card at a time, and any card that cannot be played to a foundation must be played to one of two waste heaps. Cards cannot be moved from one foundation to another, nor from one waste heap to another, but the top card of a waste heap is always available to be played to a foundation. The stock is dealt only once.

DEAL to the board thirty cards face downwards in ten packets of three cards each, and below each packet deal a card face upwards. As they occur, Aces are played to the centre as foundations.

The object of the game is to build ascending suit-sequences on the Aces to the Kings.

The ten face-upwards cards below the packets are available to be packed with cards turned from the stock, and may themselves be packed on each other, in descending sequences of alternate colour. When a space occurs in the row, the top card of the packet immediately above the space is turned face upwards and becomes available for play. The space may also be filled by any exposed card or sequence of cards. Sequences and part-sequences may be moved from one column to another, and worrying back is allowed.

The stock is dealt one card at a time to a single waste heap, the top card of which is available for play. When the stock is exhausted it is taken into hand and the three top cards are exposed on the board as a reserve. If any or all of them can be played, cards are turned from the stock to bring the number of cards in the reserve to three. The game continues in this way until either it succeeds or fails because no further play can be made and the reserve is full.

FIFTY

TAKE the first fifty cards of the pack and play the top one face upwards to the centre to indicate the foundations. Arrange the remaining forty-nine in a row of seven piles of seven cards each, the bottom six cards of each pile face downwards, the top card face upwards.

The object of the game is to release the remaining foundation cards, play them to the centre, and build on them round the corner suit-sequences.

The stock is turned three cards at a time to a single waste heap. If at the end of a deal there are only two cards in the stock they are treated as three; if there is only one card left it is transferred to the top of the pack, to become the bottom card of the first bundle of three in the next deal. The stock is dealt and redealt until either the game is won, or lost because no further move can be made.

The face-upwards cards on each pile in the lay-out are not packed on; they are available to be played to a foundation or to the waste heap, the top card of which may be packed in a descending, round-the-corner sequence of alternate colour.

When a card is taken from a pile in the lay-out, the card under it is turned face upwards and becomes available for play. When all seven cards in a pile have been played, the available space may be filled either with an exposed card from the lay-out or the top card of the waste heap.

HEADS AND TAILS

DEAL to the board eight cards face upwards in a row. Below it deal face upwards eight packets of eleven cards each. The remaining eight cards are dealt face upwards in a row below the packets.

The object of the game is to play to the centre one Ace and one King of each suit, and build ascending suit-sequences on the Aces to the Kings and descending suit-sequences on the Kings to the Aces.

Only the cards in the top row ("heads") and bottom row ("tails") are available to be played to the foundations. The cards in these two rows may also be packed on each other in ascending and/or descending round-the-corner suit-sequences.

Cards from the packets in the centre row may be used only to fill a space in the top or bottom row. The space must be filled with a card from the packet immediately above or below it, unless the packet has already been consumed, when the space may be filled by the top card of any packet in the centre row.

HEAP

REMOVE from the pack and play to the centre as foundations, a sequence of thirteen cards of alternate colour from a Seven to a Six. Deal face upwards to the board the rest of the pack in twenty-two packets of four cards each and one of three cards.

The object of the game is to build on each of the thirteen foundation cards an ascending sequence of eight cards in all; on the Seven to the Five, inclusive, each sequence is built in the same colour as the foundation card, on the Six it is built in alternate colours.

The top card of each packet is exposed and available to be played to a foundation. A card may not be moved from one packet to another, and a space made by moving all the cards of a packet to the foundations is not filled.

When all possible moves have been made, the remaining packets are gathered, shuffled and redealt in packets of four; any cards in excess of four (one, two or three) are dealt to a packet of their own. Only one redeal is allowed.

REMOVE from the pack one Ace and one King of each suit, and play them to the centre as foundations.

Deal face upwards to the board sixty-four cards in eight rows of eight cards each, the cards being laid vertically and horizontally in turn, as illustrated in the following diagram.

The object of the game is to build ascending suit-sequences on the Aces to the Kings, and descending suit-sequences on the Kings to the Aces.

Any card in the lay-out is available for play provided it has one of its narrower sides free. To illustrate, in the diagram the 2♠, 6♡, 2♢, 8♠ and J♣ in the top row are available for play; when the 2♠ has been played to the A♠-foundation the 7♣ is available for play, and when the 2♢ has been played to the A♢-foundation the 3♠ and 9♡ are free to be played.

A space made in the lay-out by the removal of a card is not filled, and no packing is allowed on the cards in the lay-out. The stock is turned one card at a time and any card that cannot be played to a foundation is played to a waste heap. Available cards in the lay-out may be packed on the top card of the waste heaps either in ascending or descending, round-the-corner suit-sequence.

The stock may be dealt twice.

REMOVE any Queen from the pack and place it face upwards on the left of the board. Deal the rest of the pack, card by card, face upwards on top of the Queen until a Queen is dealt. Place this second Queen to the right of the first and continue to deal on it until a third Queen is dealt. Proceed in this way, from Queen to Queen, until the whole pack has been dealt in eight piles with a Queen at the bottom of each.

While the deal is in progress the eight Fives and eight Sixes, as they are dealt, are played to the centre as foundations.

The object of the game is to build, irrespective of suit and colour, ascending sequences on the Fives to the Jacks and descending sequences on the Sixes to the Aces then Kings.

The top card of each pile, during the deal and after it, is available to be played to a foundation. There is no packing on the exposed cards in the layout, but if all the cards of a pile are played to a foundation, leaving a Queen exposed, any available card may be played to the Queen.

KINGS' WAY

REMOVE the eight Kings from the pack and lay them face upwards on the board in a row. Below them deal forty cards in four rows face downwards of eight cards each, and one row face upwards of eight cards.

The object of the game is to remove the forty cards, in accordance with the rules set out below, to leave the way clear to the eight Kings in the top row.

The stock is dealt one card at a time to a waste heap, and the top card of it is available to be packed either in an ascending or descending sequence of alternate colour. When a card from the bottom row of the lay-out is played to the waste heap, the card immediately above it is turned face upwards and becomes available for play.

The management of the Aces is governed by two special rules:

1. When an Ace becomes exposed in the lay-out, it may be packed on the waste heap only when a Two of an alternate colour is turned from the stock.

2. When an Ace is dealt from the stock, any Two of alternate colour in the lay-out (and subsequent sequence cards) may be packed on it, and if no Two is available the Ace, instead of being played to the waste heap, is played to a separate heap. When the stock is exhausted the number of Aces in the separate heap dictates the number of cards that may be dealt from the top of the stock in a second attempt to clear the board.

DEAL face upwards to the board as the left wing sixteen cards in four rows of four cards each, and, leaving sufficient room for the eight foundation cards in two columns of four cards each, deal face upwards to the board another sixteen cards in four rows of four cards each as the right wing.

The object of the game is to release the eight Aces as foundation cards, and build on them ascending suit-sequences to the Kings.

See diagram on page 94.

The cards in the left-hand column of the left wing and those in the right-hand column of the right wing are available to be played to the foundations, and may themselves be packed in descending sequences irrespective of suit and colour. A sequence may be moved in part or as a whole, and a card, sequence or part-sequence may be moved from one wing to the other.

In the accompanying diagram, therefore, in the left wing, the 3♡ may be packed on the 4♣, and the 2♠ on the 3♡. The sequence 4♣, 3♡, 2♠ may be packed on the 5♣ in the right wing, and the sequence 5♣, 4♣, 3♡, 2♠ may be packed either on the 6◇ in the right wing or on the 6♣ (left exposed by packing the 3♡ on the 4♣) in the left wing. And so on.

The stock is turned one card at a time, and any card that cannot be played to a foundation or packed on the lay-out is played to a single waste heap, the top card of which is always available for play.

93

When a space occurs in the lay-out, by reason of all the cards in a row up to the foundation card having been played, it may be filled only by a King.

Only one deal is allowed, but worrying back is permitted throughout the game.

LIMITED

DEAL to the board thirty-six cards face upwards in three rows of twelve cards each, the cards in the second and third rows slightly overlapping the cards above them. As they become available, play to the centre as foundations the eight Aces.

The object of the game is to build ascending suit-sequences on the Aces up to the Kings.

The bottom card of each column in the lay-out is exposed. It may be played to a foundation or packed in descending suit-sequence. Only one card at a time may be moved. A space made by moving all the cards in a column may be filled either by an exposed card from another part of the lay-out or by the top card of the waste heap.

The stock is dealt one card at a time, and any card that cannot be played to a foundation or the lay-out is played to a waste heap. The top card of the waste heap is always available for play to the lay-out or to a foundation.

When the stock has been dealt once there is a limited redeal. The stock is turned and the first four cards are dealt face upwards in a row to the board. If any of these four cards can be played to a foundation or to the lay-out its space is filled by the next card of the stock, and so on until none of the four cards can be played. The game then comes to an end.

DEAL eight cards face upwards in a row. Any Aces that occur are played to the centre as foundations, and exposed cards are packed in descending sequences of alternate colour. A vacant space may be filled only by a King or by a sequence headed by a King. When all moves have been made in the first row, a further eight cards are dealt face upwards, one card to each column overlapping the existing card at the bottom of the column, and filling any space that may occur in the lay-out. No packing or moving a card to a foundation may be made until all eight cards have been dealt. Continue in this way, making available moves after each row of eight cards is dealt, until the stock is exhausted.

The object of the game is to build ascending suit-sequences on the foundations from Aces to Kings.

When the stock has been exhausted the player may waive. That is to say, if an exposed card blocks the run of a sequence, the blocking card may be taken into the hand and held in reserve, until further moves enable the player to find a place for it in the lay-out. Waiving may be repeated as often as the player desires, but only one card at a time may be waived.

OCTAVE

DEAL to the board twenty-four cards in three rows of eight cards each, the first and second rows face downwards, the third row face upwards. For convenience the rows may overlap. As they become available, Aces are played to the centre as foundations.

The object of the game is to build ascending suit-sequences on the Aces to the Tens and following below them a row of Jacks, another of Queens and a third of Kings.

The face-upwards cards in the bottom row are available to be moved to the foundations, and may also be packed in descending sequences of alternate colour. When a card is moved from the bottom row, the face-downwards card immediately above it is turned face upwards and becomes available for play as an exposed card. Cards may be moved from one exposed card to another, and a sequence may be moved either as a whole or in part. When a column is cleared the space may be filled with any exposed card or sequence of cards.

The stock is turned one card at a time. When the stock is exhausted the waste heap is turned and the top eight cards are taken in hand as a reserve. Cards from the reserve may be used for building on the foundations or packing on the exposed cards of the lay-out. When a card in the reserve is used in this way the reserve is filled by taking into the hand the top card of the waste heap. The game comes to an end when no further move can be made and the reserve is full.

DEAL face upwards to the board twenty cards arranged in the form of a plait; that is to say, the first card is placed diagonally to the right, the second card is placed diagonally to the left and covering the lower half of the first card, the third card is placed diagonally to the right and covering the lower half of the second card, etc. A column of six cards is dealt on either side of the plait. The thirty-third card is dealt face upwards to the centre to indicate the foundations, and, as they become available, the other seven cards of the same rank.

The object of the game is to build on the foundations ascending, round-the-corner suit-sequences of thirteen cards each.

The two columns and the bottom card of the plait are available to be played to a foundation. When a card is played from one of the columns the space must be filled at once. If the top or bottom card of a column has been moved the player has the option of filling the space either with the bottom card of the plait or the top card of the stock; if any of the other eight cards in the columns has been moved the space must be filled with the top card of the stock.

The stock is dealt one card at a time, and any card that cannot be played to a foundation, or is not needed to fill a space in one of the columns, is played to a waste heap. When the stock is exhausted the waste heap is taken up and redealt. Redealing continues until the game either succeeds or loses.

ROYAL COTILLION

REMOVE from the pack one Ace and one Two of each suit, and play them to the board in two columns, the Twos on the right of the Aces. On the left of the Aces deal face upwards twelve cards in three rows of four cards each (to form the left wing), and on the right of the Twos deal face upwards sixteen cards in four rows of four cards each (to form the right wing).

See diagram on the facing page.

The object of the game is to build in suits on the Aces in the series Ace, 3, 5, 7, 9, Jack, King, 2, 4, 6, 8, 10, Queen; and on the Twos in the series 2, 4, 6, 8, 10, Queen, Ace, 3, 5, 7, 9, Jack, King.

From the left wing only the bottom card of a column may be moved to a foundation, and the space made by moving a card is not filled; from the right wing any card may be moved to a foundation, and the space made by moving a card must be filled at once either with the top card of the waste heap or the top card of the stock.

The stock is dealt one card at a time, and any card that cannot be played to a foundation or is not required to fill a space in the right wing is played to a waste heap. The game ends when the stock has been dealt once.

ROYAL PARADE

TWENTY-FOUR cards are dealt face upwards to the board in three rows of eight cards each.

The first step is to remove any Aces that may occur in the lay-out. They take no part in the game.

The second step is to arrange the cards in the lay-out so that the top row consists of the eight Twos, the middle row of the eight Threes, and the bottom row of the eight Fours.

The third step is to build up on these cards, following suit, the Fives, Eights and Jacks on the Twos; the Sixes, Nines and Queens on the Threes; and the Sevens, Tens and Kings on the Fours. Building up can only be made on a card in its proper row in the lay-out.

Suppose the original lay-out is as shown on the facing page.

Now the A♢ in row B and the A♡ in row C are discarded. The 3♡ in row A is moved to the space in row B left vacant by the A♢, and the 4♠ in row A is moved to the space in row C left vacant by the A♡. The 7♠ in row C is now built up on the 4♠. And so on.

When all moves have been made the player deals eight cards from the stock face upwards in a row as waste heaps below the lay-out. Any Aces that are dealt are rejected.

The player builds up on the cards or fills spaces in the lay-out from the waste heaps, and when all moves have been made, another eight cards are dealt

A   B   C

103

from the stock to the waste heaps, covering the previous deal.

Only the top cards on the waste heaps may be moved to the lay-out.

The game ends when the stock has been exhausted and no further moves can be made after the last eight cards have been dealt to the waste heaps.

REMOVE from the pack one Ace and one King of each suit, and play them to the board as foundations in two rows, the Kings above the Aces. Then deal face upwards to the board twelve cards, beginning above the left-hand King, in a clockwise direction, as shown in the accompanying diagram.

The object of the game is to build descending suit-sequences on the Kings to the Aces, and ascending suit-sequences on the Aces to the Kings, with the restriction that cards dealt to spaces 1, 2, 3 and 4 may

105

be played only to the King-foundations, cards dealt to spaces 7, 8, 9 and 10 may be played only to the Ace-foundations, but cards dealt to spaces 5, 6, 11 and 12 may be played either to King- or Ace-foundations.

When all moves have been made the spaces are filled with cards from the stock, and when no further moves can be made, another twelve cards are dealt from the stock to cover those cards left *in situ*.

When the stock is exhausted the restriction with regard to playing cards from the lay-out to the foundations is removed and cards may be played to the foundations from any of the twelve surrounding heaps. Further, the top card of each heap may now be packed in ascending and/or descending suit-sequence.

Two redeals (making three deals in all) are allowed. No shuffling is allowed between deals; the heaps surrounding the foundations are picked up in the order 12, 11, 10 . . . 3, 2, 1, and turned face downwards, so that the bottom card of heap 12 becomes the top card of the remade stock and will be dealt to space 1.

SENIOR WRANGLER

THE game is sometimes called Mathematics, but neither name need deter anyone; for we are introduced to nothing more difficult than simple addition and subtraction.

Suits play no part in the game; every card is taken at its pip value, the Jacks counting 11, the Queens 12 and the Kings 13.

Remove from the pack eight cards, from a Two to a Nine inclusive, and lay them in a row on the board. They play no direct part in the game; their function is to serve as indicators.

The object of the game is to release eight foundation cards and build up on them to the Kings. The foundation cards are double the value of the indicator cards, and the sequence on each is determined by adding the value of the card on the foundation to that of the indicator card. When a total exceeds thirteen, the value of the card required is obtained by subtracting thirteen from it. It is really quite simple . . .

Indicator Cards:	2	3	4	5	6	7	8	9
Foundation Cards:	4	6	8	10	Q	A	3	5

On the Four the cards are built up in the sequence Six ($4+2$), Eight ($6+2$), Ten ($8+2$) Queen 12 ($10+2$) and so on to King 13 (Jack $11+2$). On the Six the cards are built up in the sequence Nine ($6+3$), Queen 12 ($9+3$), Two (Queen $12+3=15-13$) and so on to King 13 ($10+3$). The same

107

method of addition and subtraction (where necessary) dictates the sequence of cards to be built on the other foundations.

After the eight indicator cards have been laid out, the rest of the pack is dealt face upwards to the board in eight packets of twelve cards each, one below each indicator card.

The top card of each packet is always available to be played. When all possible moves have been made, the left-hand packet (i.e. the one below the Two indicator card) is taken up and the cards dealt in turn to the top of the other packets, from left to right and beginning with the space from which the packet has been lifted. The player has the option of dealing either with the packet face upwards or face downwards.

The game is continued until no further move can be made, when the packet below the Three indicator card is taken up and the cards distributed to the other packets in the same way.

The game comes to an end when all eight packets have been dealt and no further move can be made.

If a game is brought to a successful end, the cards should be arranged as shown on the facing page.

Indicator Cards:	2	3	4	5	6	7	8	9
Foundation Cards:	4	6	8	10	Q	A	3	5

S
e
  q
    u
      e
        n
          c
            e
              C
                a
                  r
              d
            s

6	9	Q	2	5	8	J	A
8	Q	3	7	J	2	6	10
10	2	7	Q	4	9	A	6
Q	5	J	4	10	3	9	2
A	8	2	9	3	10	4	J
3	J	6	A	9	4	Q	7
5	A	10	6	2	J	7	3
7	4	A	J	8	5	2	Q
9	7	5	3	A	Q	10	8
J	10	9	8	7	6	5	4
K	K	K	K	K	K	K

SNAKE

DEAL face upwards to the board eight piles of eight cards each. Aces, as they become available, are played to the centre as foundations.

The object of the game is to build ascending suit-sequences on the foundations from Aces to Kings.

The top card of each pile is exposed, and may be packed in descending sequence irrespective of suit and colour.

The stock is turned one card at a time, and any card that cannot be played to a foundation or to an exposed card in the lay-out, is played to the left-hand pile, which, in consequence, becomes longer and longer. As it is convenient to fan the piles out, so that all the cards can be seen, the left-hand pile is commonly called the snake. The more cards in the snake, the less likely is the game to succeed. Worrying back, however, is permitted, and a sequence may be moved from one exposed card to another either as a whole or in part. A space made by moving all the cards of a pile may be filled either by a sequence or an exposed card.

DEAL to the board forty cards in four overlapping rows of ten cards each, the first, second and third rows face downwards, the fourth row face upwards.

The object of the game is to build within the lay-out descending suit-sequences from Kings to Aces. When such a sequence has been built it is removed from the lay-out, so that a successful game consists in clearing the board of all the cards.

The exposed cards at the bottom of the columns may be packed in descending sequences irrespective of suit and colour, and when a card is moved from one column to another, the face-downwards card immediately above it is turned face upwards and becomes available for play.

When a space is made by reason of all the cards having been moved from a column, it may be filled by any exposed card or sequence of cards.

When all possible moves have been made, and spaces filled, ten cards are dealt from the stock, face upwards, one to the bottom of each column overlapping the card *in situ*.

Play is continued in this way until the stock is exhausted. There is no redeal and the last deal from the stock, therefore, will be of only four cards.

[1] There are many variations of Spider, which is not so much the name of one particular game as a generic name for any game of patience in which foundation cards are not played to the centre, but sequences are built within the lay-out itself. The variation described in this book is generally considered the best with a 1 in 3 chance of success. It is mentioned in the *Redbook Magazine* as being the favourite patience game of the late President Franklin D. Roosevelt.

STEPS

DEAL one card to the board, below it two cards, then three cards, and so on down to a row of seven cards all face downwards. Finally, below the row of seven cards, deal a row of eight cards face upwards, as shown in the diagram on the facing page. For convenience the rows may overlap.

Aces, as they become available, are played to the centre as foundations, to be built on in ascending suit-sequences to the Kings.

The face-upwards cards in the bottom row of the lay-out are available to be packed in descending sequences of alternate colour and may themselves be packed on other cards in the lay-out, either singly or as sequences in whole or in part. When all the face-upwards cards in a column have been moved, the face-downwards card immediately above is turned face upwards and becomes available for play. When all the cards have been moved from a column, the space in the lay-out may be filled with any exposed card or sequence of cards.

The stock is turned one card at a time, and any card that cannot be played to a foundation or the lay-out is played to a single waste heap, the top card of which is always available for play. One redeal is allowed.

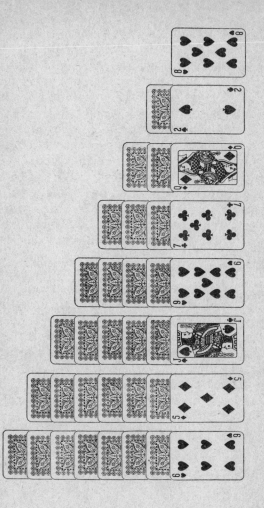

SULTAN

REMOVE the eight Kings and one Ace of Hearts from the pack and arrange them as shown in the diagram on the facing page. Then deal four cards face upwards to both sides of the centre.

The object of the game is to build on the centre (except on the King of Hearts in the middle) ascending suit-sequences up to the eight Queens.

In the illustrative diagram the 2♡ will be played on the A♡, and the A♠ on one of the K♠; for the suit-sequences on the seven Kings are round-the-corner. The spaces left vacant by playing these two cards to the centre are filled with the two top cards of the stock.

The stock is dealt one card at a time, and if it cannot be played to a sequence in the centre or is not needed to fill a space, it is played to a waste heap. The eight side cards are not built on.

When the stock is exhausted the cards in the waste heap are shuffled and dealt a second time, and a third time if necessary.

If the game succeeds the central King of Hearts (Sultan) will be surrounded by his harem of eight Queens.

SWING

REMOVE from the pack one Ace and one King of each suit, and play them to the centre as foundations. Deal face upwards to the board nine cards which, for convenience, may be arranged in three rows of three cards each.

The object of the game is to build ascending suit-sequences on the Aces and descending suit-sequences on the Kings, with the unusual condition that whenever the top cards of two foundation piles of the same suit are in sequence, any or all of the cards of one pile may be reversed onto the other with the exception of the original Ace-or King-foundation card.

The stock is turned one card at a time to a single waste heap, the top card of which, as well as the nine cards in the lay-out, is always available to be played to a foundation. When a card is played from the lay-out to a foundation, the space must be filled at once with the top card of the waste heap; failing that with the top card of the stock.

The stock may be dealt twice.

REMOVE from the pack a Queen and Jack of Hearts and play them to the centre as foundations. As they become available play to the centre as foundations the two Tens of Spades, Tens of Diamonds and Tens of Clubs.

Deal face upwards to the board sixteen cards in two rows of eight cards each.

The object of the game is to build an ascending, round-the-corner suit-sequence on the Queen of Hearts to the Jack, a descending, round-the-corner suit-sequence on the Jack of Hearts to the Queen, and descending, round-the-corner suit-sequences on the Tens to the Jacks.

The sixteen cards in the lay-out are available to be played to the foundations. When no further move can be made, another sixteen cards are dealt to cover those *in situ*, and fill any spaces that may have been left by moving cards from the lay-out to the foundations. The play is continued in this way until the whole of the stock has been dealt. Once the stock has been exhausted, whenever the play comes to a standstill, each of the piles in the lay-out (beginning with the left-hand pile in the upper row) is taken up and dealt as far as it will go, the first card being dealt to the space from which the pile has been taken. The game comes to an end when all sixteen piles have been dealt.

The patience gets its name from the fact that if it is successful a Queen of Hearts will be accompanied by seven Jacks.

TOAD IN THE HOLE

DEAL to the board twelve cards face upwards as a heel, excluding any Aces that are played to the centre as foundations.

The object of the game is to play all eight Aces to the centre and build on them ascending sequences irrespective of suit and colour up to the Kings.

Cards are turned from the stock one at a time, and any card that cannot be played to a foundation is played to any one of five waste heaps at the option of the player.

The top card of the heel and the top card of each waste heap are always available to be played to a foundation. The stock is dealt only once.

DEAL to the board, face downwards in a row, eight piles of thirteen cards each. Turn the top card of each pile and play the cards to the centre as foundation cards.

The object of the game is to build ascending, round-the-corner sequences on the eight foundation cards irrespective of suit and colour. The sequences, of course, come to and end when the cards next below the values of the foundations cards are reached.

The eight piles are turned face upwards, and the top card of each pile is available to be played to a foundation. When a card has been played to a foundation, the card under it is available to be played to a foundation, and so on. When all possible moves have been made, the left-hand pile is dealt one card at a time face upwards to the piles, beginning with the space from which it has been taken and dealing to any spaces that may have been made by reason of all the cards of a pile being moved to the foundations. When all the cards in the pile have been dealt, the game continues, and so on until each of the eight piles has been dealt once each.

TRIPLE LINE

DEAL face upwards to the board thirty-six cards in three overlapping rows of twelve cards each.

Aces, as they become available, are played to the centre as foundations, to be built on in ascending suit-sequences to the Kings.

The exposed card at the bottom of each column may be packed in descending sequence of alternate colour, and may itself be packed on an exposed card at the bottom of another column. A sequence may be moved from one exposed card to another either as a whole or in part. When all the cards have been moved from a column, the space may be filled by any exposed card or sequence of cards.

The stock is turned one card at a time, and any card that cannot be played to a foundation or the lay-out is played to a single waste heap, the top card of which is always available for play. One redeal is allowed.

TWENTY

REMOVE from the pack one Ace and one King of each suit, and play them to the centre as foundations. Deal face upwards to the board twenty cards in four rows of five cards each.

The object of the game is to build ascending suit-sequences on the Aces up to the Kings, and descending suit-sequences on the Kings down to the Aces.

Any of the twenty cards in the lay-out may be played to a foundation. When all moves have been made, the spaces are filled with cards dealt from the stock, and the game continued in this way until none of the twenty cards in the lay-out can be played to a foundation. The cards in the lay-out are then covered by twenty cards dealt from the stock, and the game is continued (filling spaces from the stock, and dealing twenty cards to cover those in the lay-out when no further move can be made) until the stock is exhausted. There is no second deal, and, of course, the final deal from the stock may consist of less than twenty cards.

TWOS

REMOVE the eight Twos from the pack and play them face upwards to the centre as foundation cards. Deal ten cards face upwards in a row below the eight Twos.

The object of the game is to build ascending suit-sequences on the foundations from Two to Ace.

The ten cards in the lay-out are packed in descending suit-sequences. The bottom card of a column is available to be played, and any or all the cards in proper sequence may be moved from one column to another. If a space occurs by reason of all the cards in a column having been played, it is filled with the top card of the stock.

The stock is turned one card at a time, and any card that cannot be played to a foundation or to the lay-out, is played to a waste heap, the top card of which may always be played to a foundation or the lay-out. The stock is dealt only once.

REMOVE any King from the pack and place it face upwards in the centre of the board. Deal face upwards two cards above it, two below it, and two on each side of it. As they become available play to the four angles the first four Aces that are dealt either in the lay-out or from the stock.

See diagram on page 124.

The object of the game is to build on the central King a descending, round-the-corner sequence of fifty-two cards regardless of suit and colour, and ascending sequences regardless of suit and colour on the four Aces up to Kings.

In the accompanying diagram the Q♡ may be played on the K♣, and then the J♣ on the Q♡. The A♡ is played to any of the four angles, either 2♠ is played on the A♡, and then the 3◇ is played on the 2♠.

A space in the lay-out is filled either with the top card of the stock or with the top card of the waste heap.

The stock is dealt one card at a time. When the stock is exhausted it is turned and if the top card can be played to a foundation the next card is turned, and so on until a card from the top of the stock cannot be played. The game then ends.

SELECTED
DOUBLE-PACK
PATIENCES
Composed by *Charles Jewell*

CROMWELL

DEAL face upwards to the board the whole pack in twenty-six fans of four cards each. As the eight Aces become available they are played to the centre as foundations.

The object of the game is to build ascending suit-sequences on the Aces to the Kings.

The top card of each fan is exposed. It may be packed in descending suit-sequence, moved to a foundation or to the exposed card of another fan if in descending suit-sequence with it. A sequence may be moved from one fan to another either as a whole or in part. A space made by reason of all the cards of a fan being moved is not filled.

Only one deal is allowed. It is to be noted, however, that unless at least one of the eight Kings is dealt at the bottom of a fan, the game cannot succeed. To obviate this, therefore, at any stage of the game the player may interchange any two cards in the lay-out.

The most important feature of the game is that with twenty-six exposed cards the player is continually faced with having to decide which of two identical cards it is better to move. Success, therefore, depends very largely on looking ahead before making a move, and sometimes it is necessary to look very far ahead. It is essential to note the position of the Kings in relation to the lower cards of the same suits. If there are two Kings at the bottom of two fans, normally the game will succeed, but the game is not always an easy one and there are plenty of traps to be avoided. By contrary, if most of the Kings are near the top of the fans, the game will be a difficult one, and very careful play will be necessary to release the lower cards under the Kings. Obviously, until the Kings are played off, the lower cards under them are immobilised. It is essential, therefore, to begin the game by looking to see if a lower card of a suit is under its own King. If it is, and in practice it occurs very often, the player must direct his efforts towards releasing the duplicate of the immobilised card. Whenever possible a card should be moved to a foundation; for cards that can be played to foundations are useless in the lay-out.

FOURTEENS

FORTY-EIGHT cards are dealt face upwards to the board in the form of an open cross, as shown in the accompanying diagram.

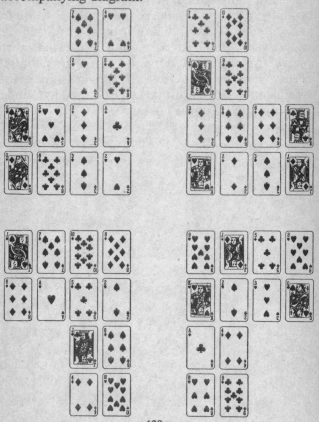

128

Ignoring suits and counting the Jacks as 11,
the Queens as 12, the Kings as 13, and the other
cards at their pip values, any two cards that touch
each other either at the sides, the corners, or top
and bottom are discarded if together they total
fourteen. When a pair of cards has been discarded
the remaining cards in the row or column are closed
up towards the centre of the lay-out. The cards
belong to the quarters of the lay-out to which they
are dealt. The lay-out, therefore, is not closed up
across the central vertical or horizontal dividing
lines, but cards that touch each other, so to speak,
across these lines may be paired and discarded. The
player is not compelled to discard a pair that touches.
When all discards have been made and the lay-out
closed up, the lay-out is completed with cards dealt
to it from the stock.

The object of the game is, of course, to discard the
whole pack.

The game calls for some considerable foresight,
and a watchful eye must be kept on the four cards at
the centre of the lay-out; for unless they can be
paired off and discarded the movement of the lay-
out towards the centre is halted. Often it is wise play
not to discard a touching pair but keep it in reserve.
Judicious pairing and discarding, coupled with skilful movements towards the centre, may help towards
getting the right card into position to dispose of a
card that is holding up the game at the centre of the
lay-out. The end game calls for exact play; for
usually it contains a number of traps into which it is
very easy for the thoughtless player to fall.

Taking the diagram on p. 128 as an illustration,

the mechanics of the game can be illustrated by consideration of the first few moves.

From the fourth quarter discard the J◇ and 3♡ and move the 5♣ and 8♡ to the left. The Q♠ may be moved either upwards or to the left; clearly it is best to move it to the left to pair it and discard it with the 2♠. The 4◇ and 9♣ are moved upwards. The K♡ and A♣ are now discarded and the 6♡ moved upwards.

From the second quarter the 3♠ and J◇ are discarded and the 6◇ and K♣ moved downwards. This allows the 6◇ (in the second quarter) to be paired and discarded with the 8♡ (in the fourth quarter) and the K♣ (in the second quarter) to be moved to the left.

And so on.

MRS. MOP

DEAL the whole pack face upwards to the board in
thirteen columns of eight cards each. The cards may
overlap. The bottom cards of the columns are exposed; they may be packed on in descending
sequences irrespective of suit and colour, and are
available to be moved to the exposed cards of other
columns. Only one card may be moved at a time
from one column to another unless two or more
cards are in suit-sequence when they must be moved
as a whole.

When a space occurs, by reason of all the cards in
a column having been moved, it may be filled either
by any one card or by a suit-sequence of cards.

The object of the game is to build within the lay-
out eight descending suit-sequences from the Kings
to the Aces.

The game is a rather deceptive one. On the surface
it looks to be fairly easy; experience, however, has
shown that it is not, and that success comes only if
the player gives considerable thought to every
move, even up to the very end of the game. The
name given to the game is appropriate; for if the
player is to succeed he must mop up a column early
in the game in order to gain a space. Without a space,
to make transfers from one column to another
easier, success is very unlikely, and if the lay-out is
such that there is only a remote chance of mopping
up even one column, it is largely a waste of time to
continue with the game.

PAGANINI[1]

DEAL the whole pack face upwards to the board in eight rows of thirteen cards each.

The object of the game is so to arrange the cards that each row consists of one suit beginning with the Ace and ending with the King. No particular row is singled out for any special suit; the player makes his own decision, and, having made it, must not alter it.

Play begins by moving one of the Aces to the extreme left of a row. It leaves a space in the lay-out which is available to be filled with the next higher card of the same suit as the card on the left of the space. The filling of a space leaves another space in the lay-out to be filled, and so on, until a run is stopped by removing a card from the right-hand side of a King. This brings a run to an end because no card is available to be played to the right of a King.

Only one deal is allowed, but the game is such a difficult one that those who prefer an easier game may allow themselves one or two redeals. In this event they should follow the rule for redealing in the parent game of Spaces (*see* p. 56).

Although there is a marked similarity between Paganini and its parent game, the fact that it is played with a double pack, instead of only a single pack, makes it considerably more difficult. To begin with, the player has to decide which one of the eight Aces he will move, and to the beginning of which of the eight rows he will move it. Then, whenever a

[1] A variation of the single-pack game Spaces (*see* p. 56).

card is moved in the lay-out there is, at all events in the early stages of the game, a choice of two cards to fill the available space. Considerable foresight is called for, because in the long run it will be found that the obvious choice does not always turn out for the best.

To which rows the Aces should be moved largely depends upon the number of cards of the same suit in the rows; usually the less the better. The object of the game and the manner of playing it demands that the cards in the rows should be either in their final places or to the right of them, but not if it can be helped to the left of them. In this connection the player must make allowance for the fact that each row begins by the Ace being moved to a space on the extreme left of the lay-out; thus as the game proceeds the whole of the lay-out is moved one space to the left so to speak.

The Kings are the biggest stumbling-blocks, but sometimes they can be left to look after themselves. If, for example, a row begins . . .

A♣   2♣   7♡   K♠   5♣   6♣   etc.

the 7♡ should be moved as soon as possible and the 3♣ put in its place. There is, however, no hurry to move the K♠ and put the 4♣ in its place. The K♠ can be left where it is until later in the game. Nothing is held up by so doing.

A row with a duplicate card in it may prove very helpful. It will be seen, for example, that if a row begins . . .

A♡   2♡   3♡   4♡   4♡   5♡   J♣   etc.

the duplicate 4♡s may prove very useful. If the second 4♡ can be moved to the other 3♡, the player can then either move the 5♡ to the first 4♡ and bring the 6♡ to the available space between the 5♡ and J♣, or he can bring the other 5♡ to the space between the first 4♡ and the 5♡, thus leaving a space elsewhere in the lay-out for an even better move.

Care must be taken to avoid getting involved in what is called a self-block. Suppose that in one row there is a 9♣ to the left of a J♠, and in another row a 10♠ to the left of a 10♣. It is clear that the J♠ and 10♠ block each other because the 10♣ cannot be moved to the 9♣ and the J♠ cannot be moved to the 10♠. The only escape is to make a space to the right of either the other 9♣ or 10♠, and though this may be possible in the early stages of the game, the more the game progresses the more difficult escape becomes.

Suppose the lay-out is as shown on the facing page.

The lay-out is not as difficult as it appears. Indeed, if the player is careful he should have no great difficulty in winning the game.

The first point to note is that although normally the player may begin a game by moving any one of the eight Aces to the extreme left of the lay-out, in this example his choice is limited to five; for three of them (the A♠ in row A, the A♡ in row F, and the first A◇ in row H) are to the immediate right of a King so that moving any one of them leaves a space that cannot be filled.

If each row is considered separately the following points emerge. In row A the 10♣ is perfectly placed; in row B the 5♡ and 6◇ are well placed, and the

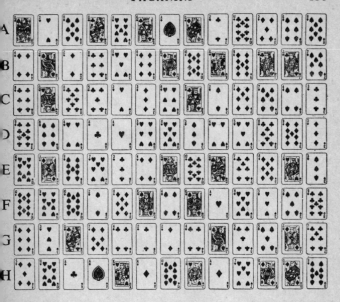

first J♣ is ideally placed; in row C the 5♣ is the only card that is well placed; in row D it is clear that, since at any time the A♣ and A♡ may be moved, there is an excellent chance of obtaining a run from the 4♡ upwards; in rows E and F no cards are well placed, and some awkward decisions will have to be made because some high cards are situated to the left of the spaces to which the low cards have to be moved; in row G the 3♡ and in row H the Q◇ are perfectly placed, and if the 9♠ on the extreme right of row H can be moved, the K◇ from row B can replace it and no longer be the nuisance that it is in the middle of a row.

At this stage the player should consider which rows

should be allotted to the suits. Row D should certainly be ear-marked for Hearts on account of the well-placed 4♡ and 6♡, and row G may provisionally be allotted to the second Heart suit because the 3♡ is *in situ* and bound to be helpful; row A is probably the best for a Club suit, owing to the position of the 10♣, and row C for the second Club suit, because the 5♣ is well placed and it should not be difficult to move the 2♡ and so make room for the 6♣; row H should be allotted to Diamonds with the Q♢ ideally placed, and row B should serve for the second Diamond suit because the 6♢ is well placed. It is to be noted, however, that in row B the 4♢ is a blocking card and there is only one 3♢ (in row C) available for unblocking; for the other 3♢ is at the extreme right of row D and, therefore, virtually useless. This leaves rows E and F for the Spade suits.

After the player has made this general survey of the lay-out and considered its possibilities the play begins:

The second A♢ in row H is moved to the space at the extreme left of this row; the Q♡ in row E is moved to the space left vacant by the A♢; and the 5♢ in row H is moved to the space left vacant by the Q♡. The space to the immediate right of the A♢ in row H may now be filled either with the 2♢ from row B or the one from row G. Consideration shows that it is best to move the one from row B so that its place can be filled by the Q♠ from row A. This way, row A may be begun by moving the A♣ from row D to the extreme left of row A, and the 2♣ in row A may be put in its proper place in the row by moving it to the space left vacant by the Q♠ . . . and so on.

PAIR FIVES[1]

DEAL face upwards to the board thirty-six cards in six rows of five cards each. If any two cards of the same rank touch each other, either at side and side, at top and bottom, or at corner and corner, they may (but not necessarily must) be discarded. If three cards touch each other the player has the right to discard which two of them he prefers. As each pair is discarded, the lay-out is closed up from bottom to top, and completed with two cards dealt from the stock to the end of the lay-out.

The game ends when the stock is exhausted, and won if the player succeeds in discarding all the cards in the pack.

It is obvious that cards of the same rank will, more often than not, be separated from each other by a number of intervening cards. Throughout the game, therefore, the player should keep in mind that for two cards to touch each other at a corner the lowest number of intervening cards must be three and the highest five; it helps him to decide which of two pairs it is better to discard first. Frequently a position will occur when a card can be discarded with either of two others. Sometimes it makes no difference which pair is discarded, but sometimes it does, and the player should always be alert to discard the pair that, if possible, will leave a further discard after the lay-out has been closed up. It is usually best to discard pairs from the bottom of the lay-out before the top; in

[1] A variation of the single-pack game Monte Carlo (*see* p. 36).

fact, since every time a discard is made, particularly when it is made from near the top, the whole of the lay-out changes by reason of its being closed up, early in the game the player need be in no hurry to discard pairs that occur in the first or second row, but prefer to keep them in reserve against a threatened stoppage later in the game.

FIFTY-TWO cards are dealt face upwards to the board, and arranged as shown in the following diagram. Between each card in the rows there is a space of one card's width.

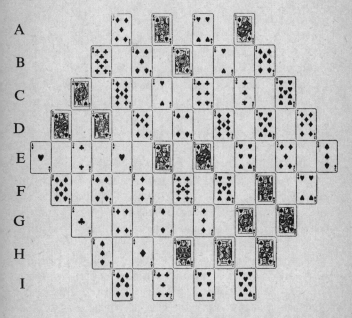

The object of the game is to release one Ace and one King of each suit, play them to the centre as

[1] This patience was composed by Colonel G. H. Latham, R.E. It is included among the compositions of Charles Jewell because it is through him that it has been made known to me.

foundations, and build ascending suit-sequences on the Aces to the Kings and descending suit-sequences on the Kings to the Aces. If at any stage of the game the top cards of two foundation piles of the same suit are in sequence, any or all of the cards of one pile may be reversed onto the other, with the exception of the original Ace-or King-foundation card.

The cards in the lay-out are subject to the following rules. A card which has two or more corners free may be lifted and played A card which has only one corner free may not be lifted and played, but may be packed on in either an ascending or descending sequence of alternate colour. A card that has no corner free may neither be lifted and played nor packed on. A sequence in the lay-out if movable may be moved as a whole but not in part, and may be reversed only onto a single card.

At any stage of the game the player may complete the lay-out by dealing cards from the stock. The cards must be dealt from the original top row of the lay-out, from left to right, and, provided there are sufficient cards left in the stock, the lay-out must be completed before any further moves are made either to the foundations or within the lay-out.

The game calls for considerable thought, because so many moves are available and every move opens the road to a number of variations. If the illustrative diagram (p. 139) is considered, it will be seen that at the start of the game the player may lift only the four cards in row A, the four cards in row I, and the A♡ and 3♠ at the ends of row E. He may also pack on these cards as well as on the two end cards of rows B, C, D, F, G, and H. Then, too, lifting one of the six corner cards of the lay-out immediately frees its neighbours. As an example, the K♠ (row A) may be lifted and played to the centre as a foundation, as also may the A♡ (row E); this frees the Q♠ (row D) that may now be played to the K♠-foundation, and, in turn, the J♡ (row C) is left free to be lifted and packed on the Q♠ (row G). Lifting and playing the A♡ to the centre as a foundation also frees the 8♠ (row F) which may be packed on the 9♡ (row C); and the A♣ (row G) is now free to be played to the centre as a foundation. And so on. The possibilities in the game are too many to continue.

ROUGE ET NOIR

DEAL to the board forty-five cards face downwards in a row of nine cards, then a row of eight cards, then a row of seven cards, and so on (dealing one card less each time) to a row of one card. The cards in each row may overlap the row above. The bottom card of each column is then turned face upwards, as shown in the diagram on the facing page.

As they become available any two black Aces and any two red Aces are played to the centre as foundations.

The object of the game is two-fold: to build on the four Ace-foundations ascending colour sequences to the Kings, and to pack within the lay-out descending sequences of alternate colour on two black Kings to black Aces and on two red Kings to red Aces.

The face-upwards card at the foot of each column is exposed. It may be played to a foundation, packed on in descending sequence of alternate colour, or moved to another exposed card in the lay-out so long as the sequential order is retained. A sequence, either as a whole or in part, may be moved from one exposed card to another, and when a complete sequence (King down to Ace) has been made within the lay-out it is taken out of the game. When a card is moved from the bottom of a column the face-downwards card immediately above it is turned face upwards and becomes available for play. A space made by moving all the cards from a column may be filled only by a King.

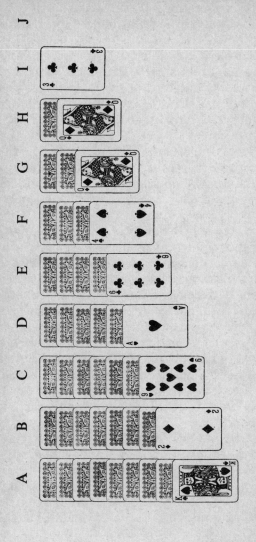

In this connection, it is to be noted that the game begins with a free space at the extreme right of the top row of cards.

When the player can make no more moves from the lay-out, or does not wish to make more, he deals face upwards one card to the foot of each column, filling any spaces in the lay-out that may have been left unfilled. Clearly the sixth and last deal will be of only nine cards.

The most important feature of this game is that the ascending sequences on the Ace-foundations clash with the descending sequences on the Kings within the lay-out. It follows, therefore, that good judgement is very necessary because the player often has to choose between playing a card to a foundation or to a sequence within the lay-out, and sometimes it may be better to do neither but leave it *in situ* to help towards clearing a column later in the game. The number of face-downwards cards in the first few left-hand columns of the lay-out usually presents difficulties. Every effort should be made to shorten them, even if sometimes it means foregoing other plays. A complete sequence (King down to Ace) within the lay-out should not be taken out of the game at once. Left in the game it may be useful to split in order to reach face-downwards cards in the lay-out.

Referring to the illustrative diagram on p. 143 the best play is to move the K♠ (column A) to the space (column J). This frees the card at the foot of column A; we may suppose it is the 5♡. The A♡ (column D) is available to be played to the centre as a foundation, but before doing this the player would be advised to

move one of the Q♦s (columns G and H) to the K♠
(column J). It is better to move the Q♦ from column
G because there are two face-downwards cards
above it as against only one above the Q♦ in column
H. If we suppose that the card now faced in column
G is the 6♠ it is of no help, and the time has come to
play the A♡ (column D) to the centre as a foundation and face the card above it. Now the 2♦ (column
B) may be played to the A♡-foundation and the
card at the foot of column B faced. And so on.

R.N.V.R.

DEAL four cards in a row face upwards to the board. If two or more cards are of the same suit, the lower-valued cards (Aces high) are discarded. If two identical cards occur, either or both may be discarded. A second row of four cards is dealt face upwards on top of the first row, and so on until the pack is exhausted. Before dealing a row of four cards, spaces made by discarding cards should be filled with cards from the top of other piles. This allows for further play before dealing the next row of four cards.

Ideally, of course, the game should result in the whole pack being discarded. It is very rare. Mr. Jewell claims that his best result was to be left with only one card on the board, and that a player may consider that he has obtained an excellent result if he is left with four cards (i.e. one of each suit).

A point to note is that there need be no hurry to move an Ace from the top of a pile into a space. A more urgent move, that will allow further discards to be made, may be preferable. Another space will allow the Ace to be moved, and, of course, there is the added chance of its duplicate being dealt.

The game is a variation of Aces Up that is played in the same way except with a single pack and, obviously, without the rule that permits of two identical cards being discarded. Mr. Jewell has chosen to call his variation R.N.V.R. because the parent game is popular in the Royal Navy.

BIBLIOGRAPHY

THIS bibliography is not exhaustive, nor is it intended to be. Rather it is a selection of those books that I have consulted. The date is that of the edition that has been consulted; it is not necessarily the date of the first or the most recent edition.

G. F. H.

Bergholt, Ernest. *New Book of Patience Games*, G. Routledge & Sons, London, 1915.
Second New Book of Patience Games, G. Routledge & Sons, London, 1915.

Cavendish, *pseud.* (i.e. Henry Jones). *Patience Games*, Thos. de la Rue & Co., London, 1890.

Dalton, Basil Imlay. *The Complete Patience Book*, Richards Press, London, 1957.

Dawson, Lawrence Hawkins. *Selected Patience Games*, W. D. & H. O. Wills, Bristol & London, 1933.

Grant, P. Francis. *Patience*, Geoffrey Bles, London, 1947.

Hannstein, Ella von. *Twenty Patience Games*, Simpkin, Marshall & Co., London, 1908.

Jones, Mary Whitmore. *A.B.C. of Patience*, Henry J. Drane, London, 1908.
Patience, L. Upcott Gill, London, 1911.

King, Tom. *Thirty-one Patience Games*, W. Foulsham & Co., London, 1927.

Lewis, Angelo John. *Selected Patience Games*, C. Goodall & Son, London, 1916.

Morehead, Albert Hodges & Mott-Smith, Geoffrey. *Complete Book of Patience*, Faber & Faber, London, 1950.

Morton, Laurence. *"The Bazaar" Book of Patience*, The Bazaar, Exchange & Mart, London, 1915.
Twelve Games of Patience, A. Rogers & Co., London, 1927.

Stanley, Bernard. *Forty Patience Games*, Universal Publications, London, 1954.

Tarbart, *pseud. Games of Patience*, Thos. de la Rue & Co., London, 1921.